A Glimpse

of

God's

Magnificent

Plans

For

His Children

ELDER WILLIAM D. HOLMES

ISBN 978-1-959895-68-8 (paperback)
ISBN 978-1-959895-67-1 (eBook)

Printed in the United States of America

WESTPOINT
PRINT AND MEDIA

CONTENTS

INTRODUCTION

In our world people live for today and very few prepare for the world to come. They are concerned for now in this world to get education, work careers, sleep, exercise, eat food, to be entertained, enjoy sex, get married, have children, grandchildren, build houses and travel. People are into having cookouts, picnics, laying on the sand at the beach, going to ballgames, races, gambling, card playing, drinking alcohol, smoking plants, going to amusement parks, and theaters. They say live your life to the fullness. So much emphasis is placed on living in this world. Very little attention is placed on worship a true and living God. Some people feel God is not real because they cannot physically see Him. Everyone wants to do their thing as long as it doesn't bother others. Almost anything goes! Live your life being prosperous in houses, money, land, vehicles and good careers. Celebrating birthdays, graduations and other parties! Others are drinking alcohol or using drugs trying to get that so call "*high*." There are some people who get involved in premarital sex which led to teen pregnancies and *deadbeat* dads! Young people focus on being highly educated in many college and doctorate degrees doing their thing with little or no reference to God or thinking about eternity.

When it comes to death people don't want to talk about it, feel at death they don't know anything because they are looking at the graveyard. Others say there is no life beyond the grave. They don't believe in *Heaven* or *Hell*. Life ends at the grave, the people say. That is why there is so much weeping, mourning at funerals for their love ones. It appears there is no more hope! It is a hopeless case. They believe the saying, "*The dead knows nothing*." They based it looking at the tombstones and quiet graves in the cemetery.

In the midst of all of this, God has plans for His children. We as born again; Holy Ghost Filled Christians have a hope when it comes to death. In this book we are going to get a glimpse of His magnificent wonders for His children. I say a glimpse because the Scripture states in **I Corinthians 2:9-10**

> But **as it is written, Eye hath not seen, nor ear heard, neither have entered into the heart of man, the things which God hath prepared for them that love him.** ¹⁰But God hath revealed *them* unto us by his Spirit:

God has given me a vision of His magnificent wonders. Take a sneak view of Heaven, look at the wonderful mysteries of God throughout His Kingdom. We will talk about the world to come and take a tour into the mighty works of God. How you like living in a world with a multitude of people with no sin or negative thought? There is no sickness or death! I will talk about worlds which dwells righteousness and no negativity whatsoever! Worlds where death and sickness does not exist! Just love, joy and peace! God is good! Good is not a big enough word to describe the glory of God. God's glory will leave all on Earth speechless! This book will give you a glimpse into this wonderful, wonderful world. May you be blessed, inspired and encourage to live for Jesus after you read this book. I am writing by the leading of the Holy Ghost.

CHAPTER 1

This World is Not Our Eternal Home

We are blessed to live in world with so much beauty. The seasons of the year are so wonderful. Springtime is when flowers buds, Butterflies and Bumblebees does their pollination process, trees began to develop leaves, birds, cats, dogs, other creatures have their young. It is time to plant for to grow new life.

Photo by <u>Beth Twist</u> from <u>FreeImages</u>

Summer is when the sun shine hot and it is time for people to do outside activities. *Fishing, riding bicycle, running, swimming, camping, vacations,* working out at *the gym.* Some go to the mountains and others go to the beach.

Photo by <u>Anissa Thompson</u> from <u>FreeImages</u>

Autumn is time for trees to shed leaves they look so beautiful. School and College starts with students getting back to their studies. Summers birds all fly away doing autumn.

Photo by <u>Beth Twist</u> from <u>FreeImages</u>

Then come winter with Christmas time, beautiful snow, ice, cold weather.

Photo by <u>Jan Zabroda</u> from <u>FreeImages</u>

All forces of nature are the handiwork of God.

You may wonder why would God allow us to have *violent storms, tornadoes, hurricanes, dust storms, droughts, volcanoes, earthquakes*? It seems so cruel for people lives to suffer or perish in such tragedies. The answer to your question is God allow these tragedies to happen because of the curse of sin that fell on the Earth through the Fall of Adam in the Garden of Eden. **Genesis 3 Chapter** It was God's original plan to have a World with no sin, sickness, animals be gentle one to another all vegetarians. The *lion, bear, shark, crocodile, wolf* and such like will not be predators but they will all eat plants, fruits and nuts. There will be no death! All animals, plants and even man will live forever! That is right! Adam, Eve and all who were born into this world were to live forever!

Question is what will happen when the Earth fills up with people? Answer why do you think those planets in the Solar System are rotating around the Sun? They are not just there taking up space. They were part of God magnificent plan to populate the Earth and all through the Solar System. God is magnificent and He is far beyond *Scientist,* *Doctors'* knowledge here on Earth. Our little knowledge is no match to God magnificent intelligence! Man can boast big things; when God wave His powerful hand, man is helpless. Just look how helpless man becomes during a natural disaster such as a tornado, earthquake, hurricane strikes it cause great destruction and man can do nothing to stop it! Just look at the wild fires in California USA and in other parts of the world. They can throw water on it but it is only a drop in the bucket for the fire is so big. Only God can put out a mass fire by sending a good soaking rain. Man is helpless! The best they can do is to try to rescue and move people out of harm's way.

God is Almighty and there is nobody that can match Him! Look how children are taught to bow down doing a Tornado drill at their school. There are adults who go into underground shelters trying to hold on to dear life! Look at how helpless man is doing a great flood. So much water that covers houses, cars, roads, yards. In order to get around people have to travel by boat or plane.

Truly *Wild Fires, Tornadoes, Typhoons, Hurricanes, Earthquakes, Volcanoes, Floods, Violent Thunderstorms* are God's way of reminding man He is Almighty and besides Him there is no other! Every since Adam sinned in the Garden of Eden our world has changed. The curse of sin fell on the entire Solar System. All the planets *Mercury, Mars, Venus, Jupiter, Saturn, Uranus, Neptune,* and *Pluto* changed into what they are today. Pluto is too cold for life; Mercury is too hot toward the Sun and the other side is too cold away from the sun. Jupiter the largest planet is full of poisonous gases. Mars, Venus, Saturn, Uranus and Neptune are not fit due to their distance and rotation from the Sun for human life.

Although before Adam sinned in the Garden of Eden. The Earth was pleasant with the Greenhouse effect by not being too hot or too cold. There was no snow, ice, violent storms, floods or even rain. God watered the Earth by sending up a mist from the deep. The Planets in the Solar System were all pleasant ready to sustain human life! The Greenhouse effect was in place throughout the Solar System.

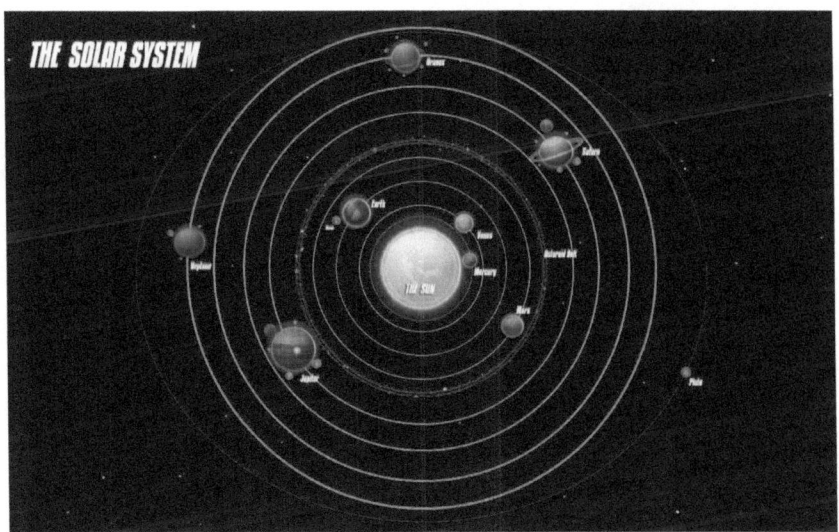

The solar system. As far as life is only proven on Earth. The other planets are empty. Do you wonder why are they there? God only knows.

The planets were NOT too hot, too cold, or there were no poisonous gases! God's magnificent wisdom empowered each planet to create its own heat or have its own shield to protect themselves from the dangerous rays of the Sun. All their rotations were perfect to sustain human life.

It was God's magnificent plan to populate the Earth with human life and when the Earth fills up transfer people to the other planets throughout the Solar System. All living Holy before the Lord God. No evil, sin, sickness, accidents or even death! This may sound crazy to you, because all you know is our Universe as it is today. The Fall of Man in the Garden of Eden cause the curse of sin to change the whole Universe under Heaven.

Just imagine our world where there is NO sin. NO war! NO coronavirus or any sickness! NO violence! There will be no police, jails, prisons, courts, judges, lawyers, doctors, hospitals, funeral homes, graveyards. People marry for life being faithful to their spouse. No adultery or divorce! Male and Female just like God commanded. There will be no *homosexuality* or *lesbianism. Common law marriage* or *fornication* will not exist. No *stealing* or *burglaries.* No *dance halls, clubs* or *casinos.* There will be no type of gambling. No type of witchcraft in any form.

Everyone loves one another regardless of their race, gender or nationality. Oh, what a beautiful time that would be! The creatures will all love each other. The lion will lay down by the lamb. All birds of the air will be vegetarians and will sing praises unto God of the Heaven. All of this sounds really good to true believers in Christ. Although in the minds of some Christians and Sinners this sounds crazy!

What they want is a world control by the **Tree of knowledge of Good and Evil.** Some people want to play a little with evil or sin. Others want to be a *homosexual, lesbian, transgender, witch or warlock* and serve God too! Some people want to commit *fornication or adultery* and be a Christian too! There are those who love to *gamble, play cards, drink alcohol, smoke tobacco or other plants.* People love boxing to see the person get bruises or bleeds from their wounds, shooting people with guns, stabbing them with swords or knives and fighting until they see blackeyes, blood coming out of someone.

People are hungry to see blood or someone beat the life out of someone!

People are hungry to see blood! They call that excitement. All of this evil in the eyes of God. That is the reason God permitted the angel of death to put an end to sin. That is the **Only reason** for the angel of death! In God there is NO such thing as Death! When Adam sin in the Garden of Eden death passed upon the human race, animal kingdom, plants the Earth itself and the Solar System. God spoke to Adam and Eve in the Garden that dust thou art and dust thou shalt return. **Genesis 3:19** The moment Adam ate of the fruit of the Tree of Knowledge of Good and Evil his blood cells begin to die and the marrow in the bone began to manufacture more blood cells to replace them. This will cause the body to continue to grow older and older. It was God's original plan for man to grow until they reach thirty-three years old. Once they reach thirty-three years old, they level off. You know this is the age of Jesus thirty-three years old. God wants all His children to be energetic. Full of youth ready to go!

Senior Citizens getting old with grey hairs, stoop over walking with canes, walkers. Those who sit around sleeping, suffering with memory, hearing or seeing loss. The natural body getting old is a reminder of God's powerful Words to Adam in the Garden of Eden. *"Dust thou art and dust thou shalt return!"*

Senior Citizens traveling getting old is a result of Adam's Disobedience unto God. Photo by <u>Anissa Thompson</u> from <u>FreeImages</u>

So, we live now looking forward to check off this planet.

This world is NOT our home! People call it home, because that is all they know! Some people have no clue what is beyond death. So, they concentrate on this world here fearing what is beyond that river of death! There are church people and clergy who preach sermons, sing songs not about the world to come or Heaven but about life here on Earth. The Saints of God would sing songs and Holiness Preachers preach sermons getting people ready for Heaven. Today Christians are concentrating on living here on this Earth fearing about the hereafter. Live in this world now with plenty *money, raising children, working your job careers, celebrating holidays, shopping, going on vacation, to the beach, camping, to the mountains, to amusement parks*. Live your life to the fullness they say. When tragedy strikes and a love one dies, they grieve like there is no hope!

It bothers me how some people *grieve, cry* and *faints* at funerals, vigils, gravesite or homegoing services. This again is the results of sin. I want to know where were they while the love one was alive? Give them their flowers now while they can smell them! Don't you know if you speak kind words and do nice things for people while they are alive it will cause them to live longer? One cause people to leave this world is they feel nobody loves them or they are just in the way! Death and life are in the power of the tongue. **Proverbs 18:21**

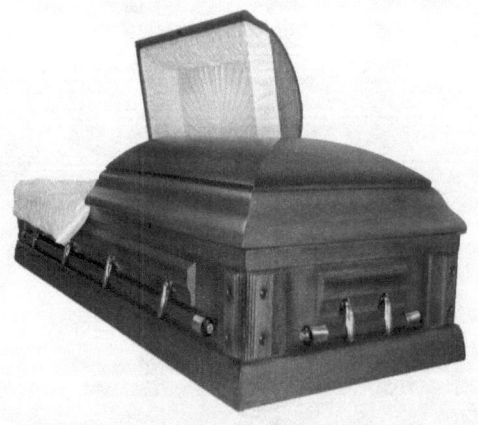

Again this was NOT God's original plan for man due
to Adam's Sin brought this curse upon man!

When you see *graveyards, funeral homes* and *morgues* those are results how Satan lied to man!

Evidence how Satan lied to man! Death and the Grave is the
result of Sin. This was NOT God's original plan for man!

Why mess with Satan anymore! He will mislead you down the Broadway into Hell Fire! Satan will offer this world in its glory: love of money, power, glory, houses, land, vehicles, sex, wonderful careers all for sixty, fifty, forty or so years! I want to say eternity is a longer time compared to forty, fifty, sixty or so years of pleasure here on this Earth. Satan uses this tactic to fool a lot of people from giving their life to Jesus. He will fool people into believing Eternity is NOT important. The Bible is a fairy tale! We need to live in this world NOW! Enjoy yourself for you are young. God place all these things in this world for you to enjoy. Jesus is just for the poor people to give them false hope! Don't fall for that trick. What Satan don't show you is the consequences to live in sin. There is no guarantee you will live all those forty, fifty, sixty or more years!

People can suddenly go off into eternity any time of day or night. Regardless to how old, young, how healthy or athletic you are it does not matter. I have heard of healthy, young man who suddenly collapse on the *basketball court or Gym floor*! Doctors are baffled! I was at the emergency room at a hospital and the paramedics brought in a sixty-five-year-old man who was in cardiac arrest. They brought him in on the air pump. The medical people worked on him to see they could get a pulse but after several negative attempts they declared him dead. Another life gone off into eternity! That is why Jesus told us to be Ready for the hour you think not the Son of man cometh. **St Matthew 24:44**

Your *education, bachelors, masters* or *doctorate degrees* does not matter. When it comes time to leave this planet people exit leaving all these material things behind. There are many times family members will fight over items a deceased love one has left behind such as *cars, houses, land, money* in *bank accounts*, whatever assets the love owned doing their life. *Greed* and *the Love* of money will cause family members to break long time relationships. Don't allow Satan to cause you to fall out with family members over the material things of this world. It is not worth it! Jesus said in **St Matthew 16:29**, "For what is a man profited, if he shall gain the whole world and lose his own soul? or what shall a man give in exchange for his soul?"

It is important to get Jesus in your soul and be filled with the blessed gift of the Holy Ghost. That is the only thing we can take with us when we take off from this planet. *We brought nothing into this world and we certainly cannot take anything away.* **I Timothy 6:7**

Having Jesus in your soul being Sanctified through the blood of Jesus and Baptized and Filled with the Holy Ghost and Fire is so important to have above all the money, education, houses, sex, silver, gold or whatever this world can afford. This takes me to the next chapter talking about God's plans for His children who love Him with all their heart and to walk each day here on Earth in the Word of God.

CHAPTER 2

Eternity

We must understand once we leave this planet, we enter into a whole new world call eternity. Eternity is without beginning or end! I stress so many people are deceived into believing life ends at the grave looking only at the lifeless body! There is no sense of *hearing, smelling, tasting, seeing or touching*. I hear of no dead person screaming in the funeral home, morgue or lifting up their eyes when they be pouring dirt into their grave. How many of you can witness a dead person screaming *"Don't put me in that grave!"*? Can you witness a dead person trying to get up out of a casket? If that was possible, I would expect people will be running out of that church or funeral home! That person is gone from this world into eternity!

There are three parts of a human the *Body Spirit* and *Soul*. The *Body* is the outer part that holds the Soul and Spirit. The *Spirit* makes the body alive. The body functions of the *digestive, respiratory, circulatory* systems are operated by the Spirit of life. The five senses of *taste, touch,* hearing, *smelling* and *seeing* are control by the Spirit of life. It motivates the body to move, breathe, think, eat and do activities. It controls your blood pressure, heartbeats, breathing rate and A1C, sugar levels. These are what the doctor checks to see there is life in the body and make sure you are healthy. When the Spirit leaves the body that is when these body functions cease and people call the person dead. The body is made from the Earth, so it returns back to the Earth.

The *Spirit* is the breath of life which comes from God the Creator of all life. A person, plant or animal when it dies the breath of life returns back to God which gave it. For the human this is whether they are saved or not! The *Soul* is the real part of the human which is in the image of God. The Soul can also see, hear, smell, taste and touch. That is true even if an injury or birth defect causes the natural body not to see, hear or walk that does not affect the *Soul.* That is the unique part of a human. That did not come from the Earth; it was created by God up in Heaven. The *Soul* is eternal and operates on its own without the *body* and *Spirit.* When the body ceases to live the soul is free to go off into eternity.

In order for the Soul to return back to God it has to be cleansed through the blood of Jesus. Sin has to be taken out! If sin is in their Soul, then it cannot enter into Heaven. The Lost soul will sink downward into the funnels of the Earth down into the depths of Hell. It will be lost in the Fires of Hell until the **Day of Judgement**. That is when God will sentence them along with Satan and the fallen angels into the Lake of Fire for eternity.

Heaven is a prepared place for a prepared people. It is God's dwelling place up beyond the Universe. Scientist states there are black holes out in space and they wonder what are through those black holes? In fact, they are wondering where is God? The Kingdom of Heaven is far beyond man's reach. They send space capsules with telescopes looking for some form of life wondering are we alone among these vast galaxies of stars? They find none because the telescope, space capsule travels so far until it gets out of range of sending back any data back to Earth! In order to get to God, we must go the way of the Bible.

Jesus said in St. John 14:6 "I am the way, the truth, and the life: no man cometh unto the Father, but by me." Jesus is the one who knows the way to Heaven. He takes all the true Saints of God who exits this planet when life ends. I want to say there are three heavens. The First heaven is what we see every day the blue sky, clouds, Sun, moon and stars. This is where birds, airplanes, helicopters and drones fly. Precipitation of *rain, ice, sleet, snow* come down upon the Earth all from the first Heaven. The next heaven is the Second Heaven this where the *Sun, moon, asteroids* and other planets resides. The stars shine down upon the Earth from the

Second Heaven. This is where Space begins and scientists sends space capsules with telescopes to see what is out there in space.

Man's technology has caused him to reach the moon! It is impossible for man to reach God's dwelling place! https://www.maxpixels.net/ Astronaut-Moon-Landing-Moon-Walk-Astronaut-Suit-60616

The Second Heaven is vast and endless. Man has no idea where it starts and where it ends.

The Third Heaven is far out of reach of Scientist or any man on Earth. The Third Heaven is where God dwells. This is the Heaven the Bible talks about. It housed the beautiful city New Jerusalem. The Third Heaven starts where the Second Heaven ends. No man-made capsule, satellite can reach this part. It takes the Holy Ghost through Jesus to travel through these parts. I am going to concentrate now on the Third Heaven where the true Saints of God goes home to live with sweet Jesus. I am writing by the leading of the Holy Ghost to give you a glimpse of God's wonderful plans for the Saints of God. Just read and be blessed!

A. Third Heaven

I want to make it plain for a true Saint of God who is truly saved from sin, sanctified through the blood of Jesus, Baptized and Filled with the Holy Ghost and Fire. There is no death; eternal life because Jesus brings life. Remember I told you in God there is no death! Sin brings forth death. **Romans 6:23** *"For the wages of sin is death; but the gift of God is eternal life through Jesus Christ our Lord."* Jesus defeated Satan at Calvary, took the sting out of death so the spirit of death has no power over a Saint of God. When it comes time for a Saint of God to go home, you just breathe out of your body. The Angel of the Lord will be waiting to carry you up through the heavens traveling until you reach the Third Heaven. Satan and thousands of demons will be watching all around the Earth and throughout the Second Heaven powerless as you fly on the Chariot of horses up into the Third Heaven. Glory! It will be a Hallelujah speaking in tongues, praising God time as you take that flight!

All of this is invisible to the natural man that is why our world lived their lives with very little belief in life beyond the grave. As far as the natural man is concerned this does not exist. They focus on living seventy, eighty, ninety or more years on the Earth and die like an animal. The natural man say, *"The dead don't know nothing."* They say that looking at the body in the casket. Then they watch it be lowered into the grave to be buried. Although for the true Saints of God they are rewarded greatly, because they believed. Jesus said in **St. John 20:29,** Jesus said unto him, "Thomas, because thou hast seen Me, thou hast believed. Blessed are they that have not seen and yet have believed."

Once you reach the Third Heaven the darkness disappears and you see the most beautiful green meadows, and the light is so bright it is seven time higher than the Sun. You look up ahead and there is the New Jerusalem so elegant, with twelve foundations walls with the names of the twelve Apostles of Jesus. (This includes Apostle Paul. The Gate post are the names of the twelve tribes of Israel.) Unlike some drawings you see here on Earth about Heaven of people in the clouds, this is in no way how it is! In fact, it is a very real world more than we are living here on this Earth! The difference will be the true Saints will be in the Spirit with their five senses and Satan with all negative thoughts will be totally cut off! Only righteousness and positive thoughts will fill your mind. It will be IMPOSSIBLE for them to think of anything negative. They are saved and save means totally cut off from Satan and all his evil schemes. Remember the verse in Revelation 22:11 "He that is unjust, let him be unjust still: and he which is filthy, let him be filthy still: and he that is righteous, let him be righteous still: and he that is holy, let him be holy still."

Here on Earth some Christians do not understand what Save really means. **Save means getting rid of sin totally. Live for Jesus, a brand new life with victory over sin. The blood of Jesus keeps you clean, pure before God and the Holy Ghost seals you up so Satan cannot contaminate your soul with sin.** You live holy for Jesus all your days and when life ends here on Earth you breathe out and the Angel of the Lord will be there to grab you. This Angel hold you fast in righteousness and you can't get away to save your life! This force is seven times stronger than the force of gravity on Earth. That is when you realize you are truly save! Satan and all those thousands of demons cannot say anything to you! It is impossible for them to speak to you because you are protected by the power of God! The Fire of God surrounds you on the Chariot of Horses.

A child of God going home on a chariot of Fire up to Heaven

You will be like a flying comet or a Fireball meteor. Flying all the way into Heaven.

Comet or Fireball meteor a signal God bringing a child
of God home! Photo by ba1976 from FreeImages

When you get there and you will see the beauties of the outside Walls of the City and foundations which are made of precious stones of *jasper, sapphire, chalcedony, emerald, sardonyx, sardius, chrysolite; beryl, topaz, chrysoprasus, jacinth* and *amethyst*. The Gates around the City are made with pearl. Three Gates in the North, Three Gates in the South, Three Gates in the East and Three Gates in the West. There are Angels at the Gates and the names of the twelve Tribes of Israel. The Walls of the City were great and high with the foundations and on the Walls were the names of the twelve Apostles. After seeing all of this, the Holy Ghost quickens and praises go out unto God speaking in tongues! Oh, it is a beautiful sight! As you approach the Gates with the Angel the Gates swings open and you see in the distance Jesus standing on the right side of the Almighty with a great smile ready to welcome you in. The soft voice saying, "Well done thou good and Faithful Servant. Come into the joys of your Lord!"

As you enter into the city other Angels greet you along with the Saints of God who are already there. They dressed you into a glorious brand-new white robe. When you put it on it cause you to shout, "*Glory! Glory! Glory! Unto the Son of God!*" This robe makes you feel so good! The Holy Ghost moves up and down your soul causing you to speak in tongues glorifying God! Golden shoes will be placed on your feet. An Angel speaks to you and say now it is time to take you to meet the Almighty God! The Angel walks you through the City and you see spectacular scenes traveling up the different levels.

Yes, there are levels in Heaven and I will talk about these different levels later. Healthy Trees that grow strong, leaves are so beautiful green. Leaves stay green all the time. If a leaf is broken it is immediately repaired. Grass is so healthy, thick and green! Beautiful to look upon and to walk on! All plant life is healthy, green, crystal clear lakes, streams and rivers. You can look and see the bottom no matter how deep they are. There is no pollution of any kind or anything to mess up this perfect scenery!

The creatures in Heaven are gentle, kind and full of love unlike any creatures on Earth. *Lions, tigers, leopards, cheetahs, jaguars, cougars* and *mountain lions* are so gentle little kids can pat them without any fear! They shall lay down beside the *lamb, sheep, antelope, deer, caribou* and *moose! Buffalo* will roam the meadows to graze all will be healthy and strong. *Wolves* along with other animals will all be vegetarians. Bears will be gentle and wonderful for the children to play with! The wild, sinful nature is not present therefore the animal kingdom is tamed and peaceful!

As the Angel travel with you through the city you observe the Saints of God traveling fast as the speed of light flying through the air! They all fly like the fantasy image *Superman, Supergirl* on Earth! The Angel spoke saying that is how we get around the city. We have no need of mechanical means of cars, buses, planes like they do on Earth! Little kids are flying through the air going and coming from School. All these sightings fascinate you so much! The Angel takes you downtown into the city and you see tall skyscrapers. They are taller than any man-made structure on Earth! The buildings are made with pure gold! You can see the Saints living in the skyscrapers and some busy decorating! The Angel walks you down one of the streets and it is transparent gold so clear, pure. Your image can be seen as you travel down the street!

The Angel continue walking you down the street you come to an intersection which is busy with Saint's walking going here and there. Some are flying through the air and others are walking fast. In Heaven there are no traffic lights or stop signs for the Saints are so full of kindness and love they give each other the right -a -way! No matter how many people there are, everyone takes their turn. Accidents do not exist! Everything is perfect! All control by the power of the Holy Ghost.

As the Angel continues to escort you to the most beautiful temple which is the Tabernacle not made with hands. It was built especially by God! This Tabernacle has giant walls made of precious stones loaded with diamonds! The Doors are made of solid gold. As the Angel approaches the mighty doors opens. Two Arc-Angels greets you with a smile and welcomes you into the Tabernacle of God. Inside the Tabernacle you see the most beautiful shining floors sparkling with gold! On the walls are testimonies of the Saints of God who suffered on Earth and prevailed for God. Those who defeated Satan and refuse to deny Christ are on the Wall of Fame for all to see. Christians who gave their heart to Christ when they were young and faithfully served Him throughout life. Their testimonies are displayed for all to see. Those who died or placed in prison testimonies for Jesus name's sake are honored on these walls. Their pictures, earthly names and locations on Earth are all displayed for all to see!

You walked down the hall admiring all the wonderful testimonies of those who prevailed over Satan. Those who Satan deceive to commit sin testimonies are NOT there! That is the reason I preach by the power of the Holy Ghost for all Christians to live right while you are here on Earth. God loves Holiness.

Living for Jesus all your days will put your name on the Wall! Satan knows this, so he will deceive many Christians here on Earth causing them to believe the lie they can be saved and still commit sin. Satan knows as along as sin is present there is no way their testimony will be listed on the Wall of Fame! The Angel escorts you further down the hall and you come to a gigantic room and the Angel speaks and tell you this is the prayer room.

You look inside the room and you see a gigantic real-life computer made up of thousands of Angels receiving messages from the traveling Angels going to and from Earth. These Angels takes the prayer request places them in a vial and deliver them to the Almighty! They are busy working traveling to the Throne Room of the Almighty and when they come out the Throne Room, will glow a very bright color of white! The Vials shine bright signifying they have been answered by God. The answers are distributed to all the Angels to make their journey back to Earth.

The Prayer Room is loaded with activities never a dull moment. All prayers of the Saints and those sinners who repent of their sins comes through the prayer room. They are delivered to God to be answered and then distributed and when the Angels travel back to Earth most get into a fight with the force of fallen angels' (demons) blocking their passage to Earth. Intense fighting goes on which could last for *days, weeks, months* or *years*. The prayer room is aware of this and monitor the activities. The Almighty looks down and see Angels fighting the demons and orders the Arc-Angels to go down and give them a hand. The Arc-Angels go down and fight the demons and this gives the Angel a chance to slip through and bring the answer to the child of God. Once the Angel gives the person the answer he quickly departs and return to get back in the fight with the Arc- Angel and give that demon a good beating!

The Angel moves you along and you walk down the hall and you see praises unto the Almighty God! Hallelujah! Glory! Bless the Lord! Many, Many Praises are displayed! Languages are spoken that God only allows in Heaven. It is forbidden to be spoken on Earth. These languages will be displayed all through the Tabernacle. As you further move down the hall you come to another gigantic room which is the Room of life. Inside this room Angels leaves Heaven with the breath of life for births in the Earth for Man, animals and other creatures. When death happens, the Angels get the breath of life and bring it back to God that gave it. Much activity goes on in this room.

The Angel escort you on until you reach the Mighty Throne Room. This Room is so elegant loaded with so much beauty that I cannot express it all in words. The doors are made of solid gold loaded with pearls. As the Angel approach the doors they open on its own accord and two Arc

Angels greet you with a smile. The Sanctuary is decorated with so much Gold along the wall and praises unto the Almighty. There is a big open space plenty of room for the Saints of God to assemble. Floors are polish shining transparent gold! The Angel move you toward the Altar to see the Mercy seat and the basin full of the blood of Jesus. After seeing this you began to shout, "*Hallelujah! Glory!*" and began quickening in the Holy Ghost! Right next to the basin full of blood is the Lambs Book of Life. This is a very large Book. This book contains the names of every true Child of God. Each name in the book of life is written in blood. Their picture goes besides their name in the book. The date and location they entered into the family of God. Only the pure in hearts name are written in the book of Life. Those who commit sin their names are blotted out of the Book. That is why I preach and teach Holiness before God. Jesus takes you from the Angel and speaks to you saying, "Come ye blessed my child and I will present you to my Father and your Father. My God and your God." Jesus takes you and present you before the Almighty! This is a greatest moment in your whole life!

B. Throne of God

Everyone must know in order to be worthy to stand before God we must be perfect, holy and no sin or negative thought be anywhere in your mind! Jesus' blood is what sanctifies taking out the old desire of sin we inherited from the fall of Adam while you are here on Earth. When a saint of God leaves this world. Jesus holds you fast Satan can no longer bring sin or any negative thought to your mind anymore! Holiness takes you over totally! That is when you truly realize what being save is all about. Praise the Lord! It is something to dance and praise God for!

You stand before God a perfect true Saint of God. The Angel who has the Book of life reads your name and you look beyond the right and you see a host of Angels, thousands of them singing in the Heavenly Choir the Song, "*Well Done Servant! Well Done!*" The Almighty orders Gabriel to sound His trumpet and signal all the heavenly host to assemble in the Sanctuary. Gabriel blows his trumpet and all the Saints and Angels rush into the Sanctuary faster than the speed of light! The Schools in

Heaven let out. Children if they are playing under the water come out. Everybody stop what they are doing and report to the Sanctuary quickly!

At God's Throne there are twenty-four elders all wearing crowns who throw their crowns down and bow before the Almighty. Two cherubim one on each side of His throne who rest not day or night crying out, *"Holy! Holy! Holy! Lord God almighty who was, is and is to come! The one and only true God."* You look at God's magnificent face which shine seven times brighter than any Sun or star! No man has seen God's face on this Earth so the mystery of God's magnificent face can be seen by those in Heaven ONLY. I am just giving you a glimpse of His glory. The look on His face will knock you off your feet. God will smile when He sees Himself in you. The Holy Ghost picks you up and you go up in a great dance before God, all of Heavenly host in the Sanctuary began to dance and shout before God. Oh, what dancing it will be all led by the Holy Ghost!

Angels will be playing the music in the Temple. *String instruments, harps, trumpets, drums, pipe organs, tambourines, and cymbals* all will be praising God. All will be dancing before God! Speaking in tongues. Praising God in the many languages of the world! So much dancing will be going on! Rejoicing another soul has entered into eternal life!

After much dancing. The Holy Ghost picks you up and stand you before the Almighty who smiles and say in a soft voice. *"Well done my child! You are here to live with me forever! You have entered into eternity! This is the real life unlike my planet Earth."*

God's Throne is so elegant dressed in pure gold decorated with diamonds and pearls. His image stretches from the Throne Room in Heaven and feet rest way down on the Earth! The Earth rotates and revolves massaging His feet! He is all knowing and can see the future! He is the Master of Science, Mathematics, History and all Education. All life starts with Him. In God there is no such thing as death! He is the God of all living. He is NOT a God of the dead! God is everywhere at the same time. He fills the whole Heaven and Earth. God knows who is in Heaven and who will be there. God knows the many souls lost in Hell Fire. There is absolutely NOTHING that God does not know!

God is the Almighty! He is the ONLY one that can create life! No other being can do such a thing! Jesus operates by the leading of His

Father! God works through His only begotten Son Jesus! Yes, being in God's presence brings so much joy! The Sanctuary will be full of the glory of God. Saints worship the Lord God in Holiness! Wave their hands Holy! Holy! Holy! Before the Lord God! The Saints bowed down and worship the Lord God along with the twenty four Elders. Then the Holy Ghost picks all them up with quickening of the Spirit! Shouting, dancing and praising God.

C. God's Name

God does have a name but it is hidden from this world. The reason is because sin invaded our world. God does not want sin in any way touch His sacred name! No sinner is permitted to speak His name! Satan or the fallen angels can no longer speak His name! We say Jesus's name is powerful which is. God's name is full of tremendous power! Just the mention of His great name will cause a massive Earthquake on the Earth which will wipe out all life. God's name is hidden from this world. When you have Christians, who speak they know God's name calling him *Jehovah* are talking in their ignorance because Jehovah is only one of God many adjectives describing His magnificent glory. He is the true God! There is a group that want to call Him the Hebrew name *YAWEH*. This only means His name is too holy to pronounce! Some call him Jesus which is fine because Jesus is the only way to Heaven. Jesus will lead you to His Father.

So, you see the people do not know and that is the way God wants it to be. Christians will not find His name out until they reach Heaven! There is no reason to waste time trying to research it out. The most important thing to receive Jesus in your heart and be Baptized, Filled with the Holy Ghost and Fire. You can be ready when Jesus comes to enter into that beautiful City in Heaven.

In the Sanctuary God shall speak to the Saints Words of life! The Holy Ghost shall fall in the Sanctuary causing all the Saints to fall out by the power drunk in the Holy Ghost! Praising God Almighty! The Angels shall all rejoice along with the twenty-four elders. The new resident at the Altar in front of the Almighty shall be rolling all on the floor by the power of the Holy Ghost! Jesus will be rejoicing on the right side of His Father! The Heavenly Choir will be singing and speaking in tongues praising God in many languages! The Angels will be dancing by the power of the Holy Ghost and others will be playing Holy Ghost music. So much dancing and speaking in Tongues. The quickening of the Spirit among the saints!

After the wonderful praise, the power of God lifts up the new Resident. The Almighty smiles at him with so much love. The Almighty speaks saying. "In you my child I am well pleased!" When the Almighty speaks those wonderful words, the Holy Ghost spins you around and knock you flat out again on the polished gold floor! All the Saints go up in a praise! The twenty-four Elders throw their crowns down and bow to worship the Almighty! Praises goes to the Almighty!

Then the Holy Ghost picks you back up! Jesus shall speak saying, "I will always be with you and will never leave you! You can think about me and here I am!" After Jesus spoke those words all of the Saints witness in one accord saying, "*AMEN!*" The Holy Ghost turns you around and you see a great number of believers all residents of Heaven. Everyone has a great big smile on their face. The Saints all receive you with a great welcome. One of the lead Saints began to sing a song of praise unto the Spotless Lamb of God Jesus Christ. All the Saints along with the twenty-four Elders began to sing a song of Worship unto Jesus! The Angels plays the music but are silent while the Saints sing their song! Glory unto the Spotless Lamb of God! Thank God for the Blood of Jesus who washed our sins away!

The Saints sing their songs in many languages and the Holy Ghost falls in the Temple. The Saints along with the twenty-four Elders began to rejoice. Jesus spread the Holy Ghost all over the Saints and they began to praise God. The Almighty sits and enjoys the Saints as they worship His Son! After the praise, all the Saints along with the twenty-four Elders fall on their knees and worship God Almighty and Jesus Christ the Spotless Lamb of God. The Angels will bow and worship the Almighty! In this the Almighty is well pleased! The Holy Ghost picks the Saints and Angels back up!

The Almighty express how pleased He is with all His creations. God shall say unto His Son, "This is my beloved Son in whom I am well pleased! Listen to Him!" All of Heaven including the Angels shall say, "*Yes my Lord, we will obey!*" This pleases God. The Saints began to wave their hands with palms in worship unto the Almighty and the Lamb of God! The Almighty shall say, "Let them go and enjoy my Kingdom!" Jesus shall say unto the Saints, "You may go now and enjoy yourselves!" All the Saints shall speak saying, "Yes my Lord, AMEN!" After speaking to each other they all disappear out of the Sanctuary to their different places throughout Heaven faster than the speed of light! The Angels all leave out to do their assigned duties. All who remain are the twenty-four Elders who sit in front of the Almighty with elegant crowns on their heads. The remaining Arc-Angels posted around the Throne.

The Saints shall speak unto one another saying,

> *Come let us walk in the park! Lets us go diving in the water to see the beautiful sea creatures and plants! Lets us go mountain climbing! Let us go and see the inside of the beautiful mansions. Let us go flying throughout the atmosphere seeing all of God's beautiful creations.* There is so much to do in Heaven and never a dull moment! They will welcome the new Saint. All new Saints after meeting the Almighty and Jesus Christ will join in with the Saints to make themselves at home!

The children attend Schools learning much education. Subjects are taught in those Schools that are not taught in the Universities here on Earth. The schools are taught by Angels! All the Saints are at the wonderful age of thirty-three which is the age of Jesus! That is the age they will remain throughout eternity! All children will grow until they reach the age of thirty-three Earth years. After which they will level off throughout eternity.

The Almighty's Throne is so elegant and He is so beautiful that all of Heaven including the Saints love so much to look at Him. The more you gaze the more beautiful it becomes! Truly the Almighty's beauty will shock this world to its very core! God's glory is so magnificent that it will cause sin and every evil thought to disintegrate. Also, God's powerful name carries so much power that each time it is used all of Heaven shakes and the creatures all bow in reverence. The Mountains quake! The Angels, Arc-Angels and Saints all bow in reverence! Even down in Hell, when God's name is spoken it knocks Satan off his throne and force him to bow! All the demons, fallen Angels with broken wings tremble with tremendous fear! It thunders loud in Hell every time God's name is spoken up in Heaven!

As I said before, God's name is hidden from this world. We will not be able to find it out until we enter into Heaven. The Godhead consist of The Almighty God who sits on the Throne. He can be seen all over Heaven. The Brightness of His face lights Heaven up with daylight. Just as an artist paint a man's smiling face in the Sun. Up in Heaven God's elegant face shines just like the Sun but seven times brighter. His clothes are white as light! His brightness will blind a human eye here on this Earth. His beauty is beyond this world and will cause the Saints to gaze for long periods of time! He is the One True God, the Almighty the Creator of Heaven and Earth.

Then there is His only begotten Son Jesus Christ the High Priest who intercedes for the people on Earth giving them a chance to repent and come to God! Jesus is a split image of his Father. His face shines as the Sun and clothes is white as light. Jesus is His Father's daily delight by dancing, singing and serving His Father!

Jesus is omnipresent in that whenever a Saint think about him or mention his name. Jesus will immediately appear. A Saint could be on the Mountain, flying in the air, diving under water, hiking in the forest or walking down the street. Just think about Jesus and there he is!

The children in school just think about Jesus here he is! Also, in School all children will be all "A" grades. There are no failures in these Schools. A child can be on break sitting near a tree and start singing a song toward God. The child's song will be carried all over Heaven and Angels, Arc-Angels and Saints will join in the Song and sing in unison unto God!

All children and adults who had handicaps on Earth such as *Siamese twins, blindness, deafness, dumbness, one* or *no legs, arms* or is *mentality retarded* when they get to Heaven, they are restored fully to be healthy kids and adults. All very intelligent than any person here on Earth. In

Heaven there are many children all races and nations who lives were cut short on Earth due to still *births, childhood sickness, accidents, birth defects, poverty, murder* and *alcohol, drug abuse.* Those young children who die of starvation in Africa. Jesus being the High Priest intervenes at death and sanctify the child when it enters Heaven, they are Holy to God's requirement. They will grow up in Heaven under the watchful eyes of God.

Heaven is so full of activities, the Saints are busy in the mansions decorating the rooms. Some are visiting their neighbors. Others are walking in a group, down the street talking. People are all over the place! The tall golden skyscrapers you look up and see a Saint of God floating on down! All of this is possible because in Heaven death does not exist! It is all eternal life! Other Saints take off and fly away just like that fantasy character on Earth they call *Superman!*

Activities will be going on until Gabriel blows His trumpet. That is when it is time to go to the Meeting around the Throne! Time for Church Service! This brings me to the next Chapter where we attend a worship service in Heaven.

CHAPTER 3

Meeting Around the Throne

It is a very busy day in Heaven and the time has come to have church. The Almighty shall speak to Gabriel, "Blow your trumpet and bring my children together that they may worship." Gabriel shall blow his trumpet and all of Heaven will quickly come to attention. All activities cease and everyone with speed faster than the speed of light rush into the temple. The Temple is filled up and the Angels filled the Choir and Music department. As you know Lucifer who was once in Heaven was in charge of the Music. He was such a beautiful being and his beauty went to his head so God threw him out along with all of those angels that agreed with him. Their places are not found up there any more!

God created another beautiful being which is so spectacular and can play music that will cause all Heaven to dance and praise God! This wonder is so devoted unto the Almighty that it plays music constantly to worship the beauty of the Almighty! The Beauty of the Almighty is so wonderful the Saints love to gaze into it! Jesus in His Priestly robes sits on His right hand. The twenty-four elders throw their crowns down and bow to worship the Almighty and Jesus Christ. Once they bow all the Saints and Angels bow in worship unto the Almighty the One true God and unto Jesus Christ His Son. The Worship goes on similar to prayer of the Christians here on Earth. In Heaven the Saints have no need to pray, so they bow in worship unto the Almighty!

After much worship, the Holy Ghost picks them up and the music began to play. The Saints and Angels began to rejoice, dancing and praising God! The Twenty-Four Elders began to dance and praise God! Outside the temple all of God's creatures on land and sea began to praise Him! Dancing and shouting by the power of the Holy Ghost. Speaking in Tongues and quickening in the Spirit. Many of the Saints are drunk in the Holy Ghost! In all of this God is well pleased!

Then Jesus called the Saints, Angels and twenty-four Elders in order! All the Saints and Angels calmed down and began to sing songs unto God! All the Saints who could sing for the Lord so elegantly on Earth is called by God to sing. Truly all the singing is inspirational unto all of Heaven. Songs are sung unto the Almighty in many languages. Then all the Saints will sing unto the Lamb of God Jesus Christ. Doing all of this the Angels will be silent but will listen with so much love!

The Saints along with the twenty-four elders will bow in worship unto the Lamb of God! Listen to the mystery to the Godhead. Both the Almighty and His only begotten Son Jesus are both one. When the Saints worship the Lamb of God, they are worshiping God in the Son. When the Holy Ghost moves the Saints, Angels, children, and all creatures it is all from the one true God! The Almighty in His magnificent beauty who sits on His Throne! I must say His elegant beauty is more than enough to captivate your eyes! It is impossible to keep from gazing at Him! The music which is played by the Angels are so elegant in worship of the most High!

The music keeps all of Heaven in the Spirit of worship unto the One True God and the Saints unto Jesus Christ. The power of the Holy Ghost through the music makes the Almighty shine with so much power witnessing He is the one True God and besides Him is no other! His power is omnipotent! All of Heaven fear and reverence Him in true love! Even down in Hell Satan and all his thousands of demon tremble with tremendous fear! They know their day of severe punishment is coming!

Saints who could sing Songs unto God while on Earth are ask to perform in the Service. These Saints sung songs unto God doing their very best. Their singing caused the Holy Ghost to stir mightily among the Heavenly host. The Holy Ghost singing and Holy Ghost music playing cause the Almighty to be pleased. The Saints then sing songs unto the Lamb of God. This also pleased the Almighty as the Saints worship the Spotless Lamb of God. The Blood of Jesus is in a silver color basin in the

Temple. The Saints pledge allegiance to the Lamb of God. Praising Him for the precious blood which cause them to be worthy to stand in the presence of the Almighty! God is Holy and all in His Kingdom is Holy. There is no other *religion, doctrine* or *cult* present. Just Holiness for God Almighty is Holy! Therefore, the Angels and Arc-Angels fly all in the Temple crying *Holy! Holy! Holy!* Lord God Almighty! The Cherubim's at God's Throne continue crying *Holy! Holy! Holy! Lord God Almighty.* The Saints also cry *Holy! Holy! Holy!* This is after the Holy Ghost songs are sung.

The worship of the Lamb of God and to the Almighty pleased God so much! The Almighty breathe out a scent of very fresh, clear, pure, cool air! This air was not like any air on Earth. This air is like a gentle breeze which satiated the Angels, Arc-Angels, twenty-four Elders and Saints of God. The Breath of God reinforce the power of eternal life among all of God's Creations throughout His mighty Kingdom. In this service it is like no church service on Earth. Saints who were talented to sing for Jesus while living on Earth are ordered to sing. Those I recognize in my vision are *Mahalia Jackson* and those who were members of my church I grew up in *Emma Jones, Frances Easter, Virginia Bennett, Anne P Jones, Mabelle Banks, Joseph Banks* to name a few and I mean a very few, because their numbers are so great! The Almighty greatly improve their voice to sing many times greater than that of beautiful voice of a mocking bird. Their singing is heard all over Heaven causing all of God's creations to reverence Him!

The Mountains, hills, trees, flowers, other plants, animals and sea creatures all reverence the Almighty in their own way! The Birds began to sing in harmony with those who are singing in the Temple. Holy Ghost music is played to further enhance the singing to the glory of God. Christian Musicians who lived on Earth for Jesus and now in Heaven God greatly improve their talents to play music totally controlled by the Holy Ghost. Beautiful, beautiful singing which edifies the Saints of God. The Angels began to glorify God while the Saints are singing. Angels join in with the Saints singing and playing music. Oh, what a glorious time!

Songs which worship God's glory, power, wisdom, majesty and His endless love and mercy are song by both Angels and Saints. The songs are no ways dry but spiritual and full of life! The music itself sings the verses to the song. Everything is in perfect harmony. The Saints in the Temple fall on their knees and worship the Almighty saying, "*Lord God we love you with all our heart, soul and mind!*" The Holy Ghost lifts them up raising Holy hands unto the Lord! All of this pleases God and He smiles so wonderful and laugh! His laughter causes the Holy Ghost to fall heavy in the Temple the Angels, Saints to dance a great dance! I mean Holy Ghost dancing quickening by the power of God! *Praises! Praises! Praises! Unto God!* Shouting to the glory of God! Drunk in the Holy Ghost! This goes on for a length of time!

The Almighty smiles and enjoys all the worship! Jesus who sits on His right side rejoices in His Father's presence. Jesus is His Father's daily delight! Jesus constantly talks to His Father. God is in deep conversation with the twenty-four Elders who sits around the Throne. When service is not in session there is much conversation going on. God is sharing with them His plans for further expanding His Kingdom. He also talks about the conditions of the Earth. I will talk about this in another chapter.

After much Holy Ghost dancing. The Angels will become silent as the Saints began to sing songs toward the Lamb of God! The songs to worship the Lamb are songs about *Calvary, the blood of Jesus, sins are forgiven* and this is one of the only times the forbidden word *sin* is mention in Heaven. The other time is doing the testimony services which I will get to later. Much singing, shouting and speaking in Tongues by the Saints as they worship the Lamb of God who sits on His Throne next to his Father. This pleases God. The Almighty smiles as the Saints worship His only begotten Son the Lord Jesus.

A. Children

Children will also join into the singing, dancing and praising God! They will sing songs unto the Almighty and honor Him with worship and praise. They will march up in front of the Saints before the Throne of the Almighty and in the presence of the Lamb. The Almighty shall look upon them with so much love! All the children bow before the Throne of the Almighty and the Lamb. Jesus who eyes are so full of love gets off His Throne and walk by laying his nail scared hands on them with blessings.

As Jesus walks by the children all fall out under the Holy Ghost speaking in tongues as the Spirit gives utterance! The power of the Holy Ghost spreads all across the Temple. The Saints and Angels all rejoice praising God. Dancing and praising God! O what a time in Glory!

The Almighty is very pleased as His Children worship Him in Holiness! The Holy Ghost picks all the children up and they march out led by an Angel to the door of the Temple. As they are marching, they will be singing unto the Lamb of God. Much praise and worship will be going on in the Temple. The Saints all fired up ready for service.

After all the praise, worship and singing comes testimony service! The Almighty enjoys hearing His children talk about His goodness. Let us talk about Testimony time up in Heaven.

Children sing the wonderful songs in Devine worship unto God and the Lamb of God Jesus https://www.maxpixel.net/

B. Testimony in Heaven

Testimonies in Heaven are not exactly like the Testimonies in Churches on Earth. On Earth Satan intervenes and cause the person to talk about what he is doing diverting the attention from the Almighty and the Lamb. How many times you heard doing a testimony service people complaining they are having a rough time either at home on the job or with their family or friend? Some complain about what is going on in church either concerning a member or the Word of God is too tight. We don't have to do all of that!

In Heaven there is none of that! The rules are simple at this: Tell the wonderful things of God and His Son the Lord Jesus Christ. This is also when the forbidden word, "*sin* and *Satan* are allowed to be spoken. Outside of singing and testimonies in the Temple toward the Lamb of God. Satan's name along with sin are banned from the vocabulary of the Saints! The Arc-Angels and Angels in Heaven only speak of Satan when they have confronted him on their journey to and from Earth. Outside of that his name is banned from their vocabulary.

Almighty loves for his children to talk about him and his only begotten Son. This is one of His favorite parts of the Service! Since the number of Saints including the children are so big in numbers, God ordered Angels to schedule them to let them know when it is their time to speak. All the Saints and children received their times. During the Service a name is called by the Angel: that person comes forth to tell their testimony. Testimonies in Heaven are unique because up there as a person share their experiences The Almighty pulls up their life from the Book of Life and show it for all to see.

Moses came up and testified about God bringing the children of Israel out of Egypt. As Moses talked the Angel showed the scenes Moses is talking about. Unlike television, movies here on Earth when God shows pictures, you will see the actual event. It will be as if you were right there in the midst watching the events actually takes place. No matter how many times Moses talked about it, always appears new to the people. The Almighty keeps all his children highly entertained. Moses testified how God drowned Pharaoh's Army in the Red Sea. The actual scene is shown the Red Sea dividing and the Children of Israel crossing. Then Pharoah's Army was chasing after them running between those waves. God show where he sent an Angel to take off their wheels on the chariot to slow them down. After when all the children of Israel made it across Moses stretched his rod across the sea and God caused the waters to come together drowning Pharoah's Egyptian Army. After seeing those real-life scenes Moses and the Heavenly Host goes up in a big dance unto God! The Angels began to dance and praise God! Hallelujah! Glory!

The Almighty laughs and sends out tremendous joy althrough the Temple! After Moses testify another witness is called. The three Hebrew boys: *Shadrach, Meshach*, and *Abednego*. came forth to testify about how God delivered them from the fiery furnace. The Angel pulls out the scene of the actual event for all to see! The Hebrew boys bound hand and foot by the soldiers and the furnace heated seven times hot! The Furnace was so hot it killed the Soldiers who were putting them in! They observed the power of the Holy Ghost who went in with Jesus to rescue the Hebrew boys taking out the heat of the flame after the fire burned their cords loose. The Hebrew boys walking around in the Fire with Jesus! The King Nebuchadnezzar testified did we not cast three men into the fire but I see four. The fourth one looks like the Son of God! After seeing that scene The Three Hebrew boys along with the Saints goes up in another dance of praise unto the Almighty and the Lamb.

The Almighty laughs and tremendous joy spreads all through the Temple. Dancing, shouting and speaking in Tongues in the Holy Ghost! This went on for all who are schedule to testify. All praising God for His mighty power. Some testified praising God for His healing power. Scenes are shown of God through His Son Jesus touching their sick body driving that disease carrying demon away. It even cases when Jesus rebuke the angel of death and cause it to flee! Scenes showing doctors shaking their heads in amazement!

It gives the Almighty so much joy when His children testify how He performed a miracle to deliver them from Satan's trap. He laughs and joy fills the temple and runs all over Heaven! I am telling you the shouting and praising God goes on in the Temple far more than any praise and worship services here on the Earth! The Angels plays music that will really motivate your soul. Anointed music that will cause the Holy Ghost to move in your soul. Every instrument you can name and those that man doesn't even know are in the temple there to give the Almighty the praise!

Even when the services are not going on in the Temple Music is played to worship the Almighty and Jesus Christ His Son. After the testimony service Jesus shall speak to the Saints the Words of Life. Jesus Words have so much power that when He speaks the Saints bow in reverence. The Angels quietly hum softly as the Son of God speaks. His

Words are absorbed like a sponge in the hearts of all the Saints. Then the Almighty began to talk to all of the Heavenly Host. When the Almighty speaks all of Heaven pause for the voice of God. There is complete silence when the Almighty began to talk: Every ear is open eager to hear what the Almighty has to say. All creatures on land and in the sea, pause as they focus on the voice of God. The Almighty will share His deep mysteries with all of Heaven. He is telling them of the future. All the Saints will speak in unison when the Almighty finish saying, "*Father, may you do all that is pleasing to your sight.*" This pleases the Almighty and he sends forth joy over the Saints in the temple. The Holy Ghost falls on the Saints their souls be quickening in the Spirit praising God in multiple languages! Children will also be dancing and praising God in multiple languages.

All throughout Heaven creatures on land and sea began to praise God in their own way! Jesus will be dancing and praising His Father along with the Saints. The Angels also are dancing and praising God in multiple languages. Holy Ghost music is played while the Heavenly host are dancing in worship toward God. What a time in glory!

You may wonder what things the Almighty has to say? God's wisdom is unlimited and there are plenty of things God needs to talk over with all His subjects. Much conversation goes on between the Almighty and the twenty-four Elders. In between services at the Temple the Almighty is in deep conversation with the Elders. God share with them many things and they observe activity here on the Earth. God listen to their input and enjoys their company!

Jesus who is His Father's delight also talks constantly to Him concerning activities on the Earth and His plans. Jesus is young thirty-three years old with blue eyes. He is so full of joy and wonderful to be around! In Heaven Jesus can be in many places at the same time just like he can on Earth. The difference up in Heaven when you think about Jesus or speak His name he suddenly appears!

After the praise, the Heavenly Host all assemble in the Temple to continue the service. Angels announces new converts who dedicated their lives to the Lord on Earth are given recognition. Their picture comes up for all to see. Jesus makes an announcement that they have been sanctified through His precious blood. An Angel signs their name in the Lambs Book of life. All Heaven hears the good news and began to rejoice in the Lord. Praising God another soul coming to this beautiful place call Heaven. During this time newcomers into the Kingdom are introduce to the family of God. A great big welcome happens which is similar to members joining the church here on Earth. Song goes *Another little lamb has join this band Not going to die no more.* The Heavenly Choir sings *Well Done* as the new members be introduced to the Almighty by Jesus. Shouting and praising God goes on!

When the announcements are finish. The Almighty will speak to the Saints and Children saying, *"You can go now and enjoy my Kingdom! Let the little ones learn as much as they can in School."* All of the Saints and children will say in unison, *"Yes! My Lord!"* After speaking to one another they vanish in a flash to many places throughout Heaven! The Angels plays music to worship God in His majesty on His Throne. The Beauty of it will cause all the Saints to gaze all throughout the service. The Music goes on in between services as well. Beautiful music constantly magnifying the Throne of the Almighty! The Four Beast full of eyes with six wings all around the Throne cries out constantly Holy! Holy! Holy! Lord God Almighty!

In the Temple, there are no seats for the Saints or children because when it's time for worship there is no time for sitting! Only the Almighty, Jesus and the twenty-four Elders can sit. They are constantly in the Temple! Now I am going to talk about daily activities in Heaven.

CHAPTER 4

Daily Activities

Heaven is in no ways like some people draw such as cartoon pictures of a Golden City up in the clouds. Heaven is an actual real world more than life here on Earth! The Golden Buildings are no cartoon figure but real life buildings. Gold paved streets are real life. Streets are busy buzzing with many people. Each passing one another saying, *"Praise the Lord! How are you?"* Respond saying, *"Enjoying Jesus Praise the Lord!"* Speaking in multiple languages goes on in the Streets among the many people. Some will be flying enjoying the wonderful scenes. Yes, up in Heaven you can fly through the air like the fantasy character on Earth *Superman!*

Saints are in their beautiful mansions decorating it to their desire. Some are hiking through the forest admiring the tall Trees, beautiful flowers, shrubs, crystal clear lakes, rivers and streams. Nice thick green grass full of life. Mountains and hills so tall and wonderful. The Hiking trails are endless and interesting each time they go. It is wonderful to go walking into the forest and sit under the tree with Apostle *Peter, James* or *John.* You look across the field and see *Moses* talking to *Abraham.* In my vision I recognize so many people in Heaven. *Joseph, Jacob, Isaac, Mark, Luke, Timothy, Paul, Mary the mother of Jesus. There are people who lived in my life time such as: RW Schambach and Sister Schambach, Johnnie Washington, Apostle TL Baylor, Bishop William Easter, Lillie P Williams, Bishop Rufus A Easter, CR Whitley, Elisha Whitley, Rosa Banks, Octavia Greene, Ocy P Easter, Nellie Green.Elnora Jarrell, Thelma Wood* and so many more! They all look so young at the age of thirty-three. There are no male and female all are as the Angels in Heaven. You can recognize them by their face! *Ruth Gorham* and *Reatha Gorham* walking and talking together. *Elizabeth Williams* under the Tree talking to *Christine Gorham. Willard Barkley, Henry Spence, Samuel Thomas, Lathan Smith all looking so good enjoying themselves.*

My natural Holy Ghost Filled mother *Lizzie Mae Holmes* grandmother *Clatie Allen and* Aunt *Missouri Drake* and my father *Floyd Holmes.* There were *Hubert Hicks* and *Sister Priscilla Hicks* along with *Masie Price! Woodrow* and *Virginia Short walking along enjoying the garden. My Uncles Matthew and Henry Allen laughing enjoying Jesus. My Aunts Della Holmes Allen and Mary Allen are there.* There was my mother-in-law *Maggie Mangum* along with her mother *Mammie Banks* walking along the trail. So many I knew I can't put all their names in my book, but it is part of the big number in which no man can number! It is a marvelous time to live in Heaven and reunite with family and friends! That is the reason it is not worth it to be fooled by Satan with the idols of this world. Although to suffer for Jesus sake in this world and forsake the idols of the world of sin you can be rewarded with the beauties of Heaven!

I am NOT racist! I love All people regardless of their skin color. I can say there are many, many black people throughout Heaven. Those who suffered so badly on Earth due to *poverty, sickness, slavery* and *child abuse.* There are Jews who suffered badly killed in *concentration camps ovens, poisonous gas showers, starvation* by Hitler doing World War II.

This is some of the horrors of World War II toward the Jews.
Photo by Mihai Gubandru "https://freeimages.com

These people secretly believed in Jesus doing their horrible life on Earth. When they died Jesus intervened sanctified them and filled them with the Holy Ghost to get them ready for Heaven. There are those former Muslims in Heaven while on Earth secretly denounce their false religion and believed on Jesus as the Savior of the World. Those with *down syndrome* on Earth will be in Heaven but the illness will not because Jesus would have healed, saved them. Those adults who suffered on Earth with other handicaps will be there if they believe on Jesus as their Savior.

So peaceful throughout the meadow and not a problem in the air! As you hike along the trail, you hear birds singing praises unto God in their own way. *Sheep, wildebeests, zebras, antelopes, ostriches, buffaloes* all graze in the field. All of God's creations are friendly and easy to be around. Animals where on Earth are predators and scary to be around are gentle, kind and eat grass. *Lions, tigers, wild dogs, leopards, cheetahs* are all kind, gentle and easy to be around. In these meadows you witness the lion laying down by the lamb. As you walk along someone in the valley start singing a song unto God. You began to sing and the animals began to worship their own way. All the saints in the meadow stop their conversation and join into the song. Those Saints in their mansions join into the singing. Those walking the streets also began singing. The children in the schools take a break from their studies and start singing. The Angels join into the song and sing with all their heart unto the Almighty. Praising God in His mighty glory! His Throne is a great sight to see! It causes all of Heaven to love to gaze! All of Heaven is full of light bright as day! The Light comes from the Throne of God! The singing goes up to the Almighty, who is very pleased and blesses all of those who worship Him! I tell you people sing in Heaven because they want to sing. God loves free will and in Heaven all of God's subjects do what they do for Him because they want to do it! They truly love God so much with all their heart.

The Saints walks thru the meadows talking about Jesus! Each time they mention Jesus He appears right there with them. No matter where you be in Heaven up on the mountain, down in the valley, at the rivers or in the water. You mention the name Jesus and He appears right there with you! When the Saints talk among themselves about Jesus and say good things about Him. Jesus suddenly appears and say, "Thank you for saying those nice things about me!" The Saints have wonderful conversations hiking in the Meadow up the Mountains and down in the valley. I saw *Bro. Hubert Hicks* talking with *Bro Woodrow Short* and *Minister Clarence Jones*. *Bishop Charlie Parker* talking to *Deacon Sandy Miles*! *Overseer Robert L Easter* walking with *Bro. Josh Boone* and another saint. All just enjoying God's beautiful creations. Nothing negative, no bad thoughts, bad feelings just a perfect atmosphere!

In Heaven your eyesight and hearing are phenomenal in that they can see further than 20/20. You will be able to read the smallest words many miles away. Also, you will be able to hear the smallest noise many miles away. If someone whispers many miles away you will be able to hear and understand! So much love in the air and it is impossible for the Saints to think any negative thoughts. Jesus has them saved. If it be any possibility for something negative to invade their thoughts Jesus will suddenly appear to clear it up! The Saints are saved! They all belong to Jesus Christ! Sin or negativity can no longer invade their thoughts!

High on the mountains you can see way into the valleys and observe all the animals grazing in the fields. You can sit at the edge with no fear of falling off. If you step off the edge the Holy Ghost will cause you to glide down to safety! Remember there is no death up there! All the vegetation is thick, green, and healthy. There are no sick or weak plants. Trees are tall just like the building downtown. Saints can climb trees and float all the way down! Saints can just sail through the air and enjoy the scenes below. Fly like the birds. All activity is under the watchful eye of the Almighty! *Isaiah* the prophet is hiking through the mountains. *Jeremiah, Haggi, Hosea, Malachi* and *Daniel* all hiking together through the Meadows. So much beauty, peace and full of love.

All the Saints enjoy each other company ALL the time! They NEVER get tired! The Love of God is mighty strong! Just like I stress, any thought of evil, bad feeling, sickness don't even exist! The Angels flying around Heaven enjoy talking to the Saints. Even God's Mighty Throne is open for those to drop by and visit between services. God loves the company of His children. God in His mighty wisdom will send the Holy Ghost in the form of a beautiful rainbow throughout Heaven to pick up someone He wants to visit. The Rainbow picks up the Saint and brings them in faster than the speed of light!

A. Visiting with The Almighty

Fantastic Rainbow around the Throne of the Almighty!

The Holy Ghost Filled Colorful Rainbow brings you quickly in the presence of the Almighty. A wonderful smile is on His face as He speaks to you. God makes you feel so comfortable that you don't have to fear! The four Beast all full of eyes crying "*Holy! Holy! Holy! Lord God Almighty which was, is and is to come.*" and the Twenty-four Elders are present. The Holy Ghost speaks in you saying, God speaks,

> "*It is good to see you! Come and take a seat. How do you like my Kingdom?* Do you have any suggestions to add to my wonderful Kingdom?" You respond saying "*My Lord, Your Kingdom is so wonderful and I am still enjoying what you already have created! Glory!*" You began to praise God! The Almighty laughs and says, "*It pleases me you are enjoying my Kingdom. I have greater plans for all my children in which I will share with you all. I am a God full of Life, love, joy, peace and goodness!*"

Many, many things God talks to you about. The twenty-four Elders are full of conversation as well. Jesus sitting on the right-side joins in the conversation. Jesus speaks *"It is my Father's good pleasure to give you the treasures of the Kingdom."* You respond, *"Yes, my Lord I am really having a marvelous time."* This pleases the Almighty so much!

God talks constantly to the twenty -four elders getting their input on His many Future plans. You may ask, If God is all knowing why does He ask the twenty-four elders or the Saints? Great question! Answer: God loves dialogue. It pleases the Almighty for His creation to communicate with Him. So, visitation with the Almighty is a very important event in Heaven. It is a very exciting time for the Saints. Doing the visit music is played in worship to the Almighty. A great colorful rainbow shines around the Throne! Arc- Angels who encircle the Throne stand at attention ready to be dispatch when God speaks to them.

B. The Mind of God

God's mind is far above our human mind on Earth Our mind we can only hold a conversation with one person at a time. It is very difficult to carry on two or more conversations with different people at the same time. This is not at all hard with God. God can be talking very intelligently to you and all the Heavenly Host. Then at the very same time be engage in millions and millions of conversations going on with individuals throughout the Earth. This is amazing! Everyone has His direct attention! That is amazing for no human being can understand this great mystery of God.

Truly God's glory captivates all of Heaven! He shines with so much wonder and amazement! The colors are marvelous. All colors are so bright and flashes seven time brighter than lights on Earth. It is far more beautiful than any man decorated Christmas Tree on Earth!

All colors come from God. Who is the Great Creator of all colors! Tibor Fazakas from FreeImages

The music that is playing reinforce His glory, power and majesty. The origin of all life resides there. The creation of all things resides there. The secrets how Man can be formed out of the dust of the Earth along with plants and animals are found in the glory of God. All education, knowledge, wisdom can be found there.

Spirit of Time for past, present and future are also there. Whatever is going on in Earth, throughout Space, under the Earth and down in Hell is all there. People thoughts, ideas, sayings and doings are all recorded. Every human being life from the womb to the grave is already recorded. The life of all plants and animals are recorded from birth to death. God is all knowing, so He knows the future! He is the future. In God's glory you can see the origin of stars how they are created and burn continuously without going out. The origin of the Sun, moon, planets, comets and asteroids are all there.

Photo by William Picard from FreeImages

The Sun that shines continuous rotating on its axis secrets of its magnificent creation is found in God's glory!

Scientist on Earth only has theories; God has the exact facts! There are many, many things natural man does not know. They will discover new technology as much as the Almighty allows him.

Spirit of all languages is there. There are languages spoken ONLY in Heaven that are forbidden to be spoken on Earth. God shall empower all His children to speak all languages fluently. As a person visits the Almighty, they observe activity going on in the Earth. All the evil, violence, war, crime going on they know all about it. They will see activity going on throughout Space. They even see the lost souls burning down in Hell and Satan sitting on his throne. Demons tormenting the souls. They hear all that going on and can even understand their thoughts. It is a wonderful treat to be in His presence and to observe all these wonders. A visit with the Almighty is a privilege beyond this world. That is why at service time the Saints rush in before the Almighty because there is so much joy, love and happiness!

Jesus who sits on His throne on the Right side controls the Earth for His Father. He serves as the High Priest interceding for the souls of men and women. God is all knowing the span of Earth from the time of creation to the time He will say, "It is enough! Send my Son to bring my Children home!" Only God knows that time.

That is why Jesus said in St. Matthew 24:36 *"But of that day and hour knoweth no man, no, not the angels of heaven, but my Father only."* I want to set the record straight. God commanded me NOT to debate with my sisters and brothers in the *Apostolic Faith Church of Jesus* who believe in Jesus only in the Godhead. God knows no man has seen God at any time in this world and live. St John 1:18 *"No man hath seen God at any time, the only begotten Son, which is in the bosom of the Father, he hath declared him."* They say Jesus is God. That is alright, because God in Heaven knows the people does not know. God told me if you live Holy each day. Love the Lord living free from sin. When they get to Heaven, He will straighten them out! They will see the Godhead in Heaven and will be amazed! The matter will quickly disappear!

It is Satan who wants Church people to argue over matters that really does not help a person enter into Heaven. We need to make peace one with the other and live holy before God, so we can enter into this beautiful City in Heaven. I am NOT talking about three gods! I am talking by the leading of the Holy Ghost saying there is but ONE true God! There is His only begotten Son our Lord and Savior Jesus Christ! The Holy Ghost with Fire which flies all over Heaven and fills the hearts of the true Saints of God. All of these make up the ONE True God in the Godhead.

Visiting with the Almighty is so wonderful. God will send the rainbow all around Heaven to pick up His children for a visit. This goes on continuous between worship Services. All in Heaven eagerly waits for their chance for a personal visit with the Almighty.

CHAPTER 5

Three Levels of Heaven

Against the belief of some Christians the Lord God let me know there are three levels in Heaven. Now I understand why those sanctified, Holy Ghost Filled clergy preached strict Holiness because the more a believer love the Lord enough to give up the world the greater their reward will be in Heaven. God loves for His children to dedicate their whole life unto Him while on Earth. That is to go through life and don't taste no alcoholic drinks, no smoking any plants, no use of profanity or swearing. No stealing, lying, hatred, fornication, adultery, dancing at the clubs or use of witchcraft. No Homosexuality or Lesbianism and marriage to a single man or woman for life. It is true that every believer in Christ will get their one penny which is eternal life in Heaven. Once you get into Heaven there are rewards and surprises that God has for all His children.

I will explain in clarity how these three levels works:

A. Level One

This level is the first one you will come to at the Gates of Heaven. Once those beautiful gates open you will see the beautiful green meadows, crystal clear streams and lakes. Trees looks so healthy, tall and strong. Animals roam freely. So much peace and love. The Saints will gather to meet new comers. Angels will come to dress all new comers with their glorious white robe and the route will began to march them to meet

God. The Almighty smiling face can be seen clear in the distance along with Jesus sitting on His right hand.

This level all of those who dedicated their life to Jesus before they departed this world are assigned here. Reason they were given multiple opportunities to dedicate their life to Jesus. They refuse and said they rather enjoy the pleasures of sin. They enjoyed sin and when they finally saw death and was given one last time to repent, they surrendered unto God. By the Grace of God, they just made it into Heaven! They will be dressed in a glorious white robe and escorted to meet the Almighty. After the visit they will be assigned to the first level. There they will decorate the buildings which is made of precious stones. The First level is so beautiful. All live together in much love and peace! Those who are assigned there can visit all over Heaven, they must return to the level they are assigned. It is on that level when every soul will say, *"You just made it in!"*

B. Second Level

This Level housed all those believers who dedicated their lives unto God. Although doing their Christian walk with Christ they disputed strong teachings of the Holiness of God. They feel they can serve God enjoying the world too contradicting what Jesus said in **St. Matthew 6:24**

> No man can serve two masters: for either he will hate the one, and love the other; or else he will hold to the one, and despise the other. Ye cannot serve God and mammon.

It grieved the Holy Ghost they tried to ignore what Jesus said. God sent His clergies to warn them to repent but they disputed those clergies and others walked out the church to follow clergies who allowed the *demonic spirit of Jezebel* to seduce them to disobedience to God's Word.

These individuals disputed the Bible in **I Peter 3:3** *Whose adorning let it not be that outward adorning of plaiting the hair, and of wearing of gold, or of putting on of apparel;*

I Timothy 2:9

In like manner also, that women adorn themselves in modest apparel, with shamefacedness and sobriety; not with broided hair, or gold, or pearls, or costly array;

They gave in to Satan and dressed just like the sinners in gold earrings, necklaces, lip stick and other women dressed in pants looking like a man in violation of what God commanded in **Deuteronomy 22:5**

The woman shall not wear that which pertaineth unto a man, neither shall a man put on a woman's garment: for all that do so are abomination unto the LORD thy God.

There are those men who are there who disobeyed the Word of the God when God commanded through Apostle Paul that a man should not wear long hair like a woman for it is ashamed unto him **I Corinthians 11:14**

Doth not even nature itself teach you, that, if a man have long hair, it is a shame unto him?

When these individuals did these things, it grieved the Holy Ghost. They were given multiple opportunities to repent and change their behavior while on Earth; they refuse given heed to that Jezebel demonic spirit in clergies which lied unto them saying, "*It is no harm. That Scripture does not mean that! You are under the Nazarite vow.*"

Clergies are there who live Holy for Jesus and preached the Gospel with the Holy Ghost & Fire but they gave in to that Jezebel demon and seduced some of God's children to the spirit of whoredom by allowing them to dress like sinners who don't know God. They allowed God's children to put on *earrings, lipstick, gold, necklaces* and the women wear pants like a man. They even allowed men to wear long hair like a woman. When warned of God through faithful clergies and in dreams. They ignored it and gave heed to that Jezebel demon to continue to mislead God's people. This grieved the Holy Ghost. Therefore, the righteous demands of a just God are not totally satisfied. By Grace through Jesus Christ and their faithful living in Holiness cause them to enter into Heaven. They will be assigned to the Second Level of Heaven.

There will be those there who lived holy for God, but they listen to Satan endorsing education, prosperity and they idolize education, money, houses, cars more than God. This grieved the Holy Ghost. God gave them multiple times to repent while on Earth, but they refuse.

Since they fell into that lie of Satan. Although they lived a Holy life before God. God's Grace through His begotten Son Jesus allowed them into Heaven to be assigned to the Second level.

The Second level just like the first level is so beautiful with crystal clear streams, lakes, rivers and green meadows. The buildings are beautiful made with precious stones. The trees are so tall and beautiful and flowers are so lovely. The grass is green and stay at the right height all over Heaven. It never needs mowing. Animals roam freely all through the different levels of Heaven. Angels fly from one level to the other level.

C. Third Level

This is the level for a True Saint who suffered for God not giving into Satan temptations. Those who suffered a martyred death for Jesus. They lived free from sin serving God from their youth all the way until they were old without compromising for sin. Saints who fasted and prayed unto God forsaking the amusement parks, ballgames, lying nearly nude on the beaches, but dressed holy to lift up the name of sweet Jesus. They shout, dance and praised God in righteousness and Holiness. Many times, they shed tears trying to hold on to Jesus and not deny Him. They fed the hungry, visit the sick, went to those who were in prison, gave water to the thirsty, shelter to the homeless.

This part of Heaven is also called the **New Jerusalem** which housed the Temple of God. There are tall gold buildings and shinning streets paved in solid gold! Everything shinning so bright and God's smiling face shines up in the sky seven times brighter than the Sun.

They will enter into the most beautiful, elegant part of Heaven with those gorgeous mansions. A beautiful mansion with their name on it is ready for them to move in. The mansion is made of solid gold and silver embedded all through it. Polish gold floors on the inside along with the gold walls. The Furniture will be so elegant made with the finest materials. When I see all those elegant mansions built in solid gold. On the inside Angels flying in and out bringing all that you need to decorate your mansion.

These things are so wonderful, I can understand now why those old time Holiness clergies teach and preach strict holiness like they did while on Earth. I understand why the Holy people taught against playing the lottery, gambling and all card playing. I understood why they taught against women wearing pants, jewelry, lipstick and make-up and men wearing long hair. I also understood why they taught against going to amusements parks and ballgames.

You suffer in this world now so you can enjoy the riches for eternity up in Heaven. That is how the Saints will say, "*Just one moment in God's Kingdom will pay for it all.*" All of the suffering and going without the pleasures of this world will be far worth it! Satan has fooled too many Christians into enjoying the world and say they will get the riches in Heaven something they don't deserve. They are in for a rude awakening! You will get your one penny of eternal life as Jesus says. As far as the mansions are, they are prepared for those who suffered for Jesus name's sake. Christians who were fooled by Satan and enjoyed the world of prosperity now on Earth will miss out on the mansions up in Heaven.

Those Christians who say they will get what they don't deserve will be on the first and second levels of Heaven. Based upon the life they lived on Earth they spoke the truth when they said, "*They get what they don't deserve!*" Those who truly love the Lord with all their heart will reach the third level. They will get all they deserve! They suffer for Christ and now they will reign with Christ. In Heaven there will be no *covetous, jealousies, envies* or *strife*. Everybody will be glad and excited for everyone. Just to enter into those beautiful Gates are a very High honor! Most important to escape the horrors of Hell is something to be glad about throughout eternity!

I will go over the levels of Heaven again later in my book and explain them more in detail. I understand some Christians don't believe it, but it does not make it not true. I am writing by the inspiration of the Holy Ghost. Heaven is more than what people say here on Earth. If you love the Lord and live a life in the world free from sin. God will honor you highly in Heaven. If a Christian live a life doing things grieving the Holy Ghost, then their chances of reaching a higher level in Heaven will diminish. Satan knows this! That is why he encourages Christians to do things questionable in the Word of God. Christians feels some things are man's ideas. This is a trick Satan uses to lure many Christians into worldly habits which is against the Word of God.

Visiting will be such a busy time up in Heaven. The first, second and third level people visit one another. There is so much love and fellowship. The Saints will continuously say to each other, *"I am so glad for you!"* They will love each other as Jesus commanded. Those on the First and Second level will rejoice with those on the Third level. Just like I said, there will be no jealousy, covetous spirit or any negative feelings. Just joy, peace, and love for each other. Everyone will be happy for each other!

Everyone in Heaven will be dressed in a glorious white robe signifying Holiness unto the Lord. The robe will ALWAYS stay new and clean! It will NEVER get dirty no matter how much they wear it! They will have golden shoes which will be the best shoes they ever worn! They are comfortable, light and easy to travel. Each child of God will be given a crown of life to wear on their head signifying eternal life! Those who love the Lord so much to bring souls to Christ will have stars decorated on their crown.

A crown of life given to every child of God in Heaven. A symbol of eternal life with sweet Jesus. Photo by <u>Jeff Miller</u> from <u>FreeImages</u>

I see so many of the Saints who were great clergies on Earth who won many souls for Jesus. Their crown is heavily decorated with stars! These stars are real just like the stars that shine out in space! They shine bright that the natural eyes cannot stand to look at it! It will immediately blind the natural eyes. Also the intensity of the heat will be far too hot for the natural man! Although for the Saints of God, it is just a cool breeze! O how beautiful it is!

Activity on the first and second levels are busy with the Saints decorating their living quarters working together as a team. No dispute does not even exist! No negative thought will ever come into their mind for Satan is not there! They will always be glad to see each other and will NEVER get tired of their fellow Saints. Jesus will appear anytime they mention His name! As the Saints look up in the sky, they can see the Almighty smiling face shine in the distance! Praise and worship shall come from the Saints on the first and second levels which will reach the third level and all of Heaven will join in the praise and worship to the Almighty! BLESS BE THE LORD GOD ALMIGHTY!

Angels shall fly constantly from the first, second and third levels of Heaven crying *Holy, Holy, Holy, Holy Lord God Almighty*! Their sound shall be beautiful music in the ears of the Saints. The wonderful sounds of children laughing, running around playing all around the first, second and third levels. There are many children in Heaven. Children of all races, languages and nations of the Earth. They love each other and there is no dispute, argument, or any misunderstanding. Peace in the valley!

Children play in so much love all throughout Heaven
Photo by Afonso Lima from FreeImages

The children play all throughout the meadow on the lakes under the water, up in the mountains and in depths of the rivers. No matter where they are it is under the watchful eyes of Almighty God. They go into the water and when they come out their clothes will immediately dry out! They play in the sand and don't get dirty! Their clothes will ALWAYS stay clean and brand new!

School bells ring throughout Heaven signal it is time for school all the children rush into the classroom to begin their studies. The Angels are present ready to start class. Subjects are taught in these schools which NOT taught here on the Earth such as other solar systems in the galaxy.

The Angels take their classes on field trips visiting these distance worlds. I will talk about this in detail later in my book. Mathematics in depth is taught solving very complex problems which qualifies for Trigonometry. Fractions, decimals, and percentages are all taught. Science is taught in depth explaining the origin of Life. Teaching different formulars in Chemistry. The Children shall observe the Almighty in the Throne Room create life. The Schools are all full of Activity! Never a dull moment!

The schools in Heaven are full of activity. Never a dull moment! Photo by Gokhan Okur from FreeImages

So much activity goes on throughout the Kingdom of Heaven. There are many people, animals, plants and Angels. Joy and excitement flood the air! All the Saints feels good they made it! No more will they have to worry about Satan and all the sin and troubles of this world. They are to live with sweet Jesus forever throughout eternity! Glory! Glory! Glory!

On all levels of Heaven there are places prepared for all those who are on their way to Heaven. Just like on Earth people have graveyard or cemeteries to remind people of those who once lived on the Earth. In

Heaven it is the opposite those Saints who have not yet entered Heaven name is written on their mansion or place prepared for them. It will be waiting for them to arrive. The Saints, who are already in Heaven, view it just like those who view those in the graveyards or cemeteries on Earth. The Saints are waiting for those believers to come in! You must know up in Heaven God is the Master of all time. Every human being, plant and animal life span is already planned out in the eyes of God. God knows the future. God is the one who can extend time or shorten time on anyone's life.

I understand sinners and some Christians will dispute me on this, because they feel if they practice good health measures, eat right, exercise, sleep and don't worry it will help their lifespan. This is true but what about the factors you cannot control such as car accidents, hurricanes, tornados or other natural disasters?

So, it is a God who controls all time! If God says you will live. A person will live regardless what the doctor or medical profession says. On the other hand, if God says the person will die a perfectly healthy person could drop dead. Medical Science is baffled. These things go on in the Mysteries of God.

CHAPTER 6

The Mysteries of God

God is full of amazement which will blow your mind. As He sits on His Throne of elegance all power is in His hands. All activity which goes on the Earth is control by God as far as life is concern. What God did not authorize is sin, sickness, evil and death. **God only allowed the law of death to put an end to sin!** All of this came about because of the fallen angel Satan and those thousands and thousands of demons which run all through the Earth causing havoc. The eyes of the Lord run to and fro throughout the whole Earth beholding the good and the evil. God is holy and He loves to see righteousness all the time. It displeases God to see all the violence which goes on throughout the Earth. People are robbing, stealing, sexual assaults, worshiping false religions, idols, practicing witchcraft, committing adultery and fornication. Other feels there is no God, and the bible does not apply to them in this day. We can do as we please.

God permit the law of man to be a controlling agent to hold down so much evil. This explains the reason we have police officers, military, jails, lawyers, judges in court of law, correctional facilities to help control the wickedness of this world.

God permit the Police to be a force to control the violence here on the Earth! https://www.maxpixel.net/
Police-Cops-Police-Car-Task-Force-Squad-Car-3274553

Satan has corrupted the law of man that it is not perfect to control all evil. In fact, some laws are against the Will of God such as legalizing the use of marijuana for people to get high or drunk. The use of tobacco plant for people to smoke or chew. Satan has corrupt man to make laws violating God's sacred law of male & female in a marriage into man marrying another man and a woman marrying another woman.

We cannot physically see the Almighty God because God hid himself due to sin. People will use this as an excuse to be disobedient to the Almighty. What they fail to realize although the Almighty is invisible to them, but He stills sees them in their sins. God sees people in their secret chambers; He understands their thoughts. He can see through solid doors, night and day is just the same to Him. If people could see God's eyes watching them they would straighten up their way of living.

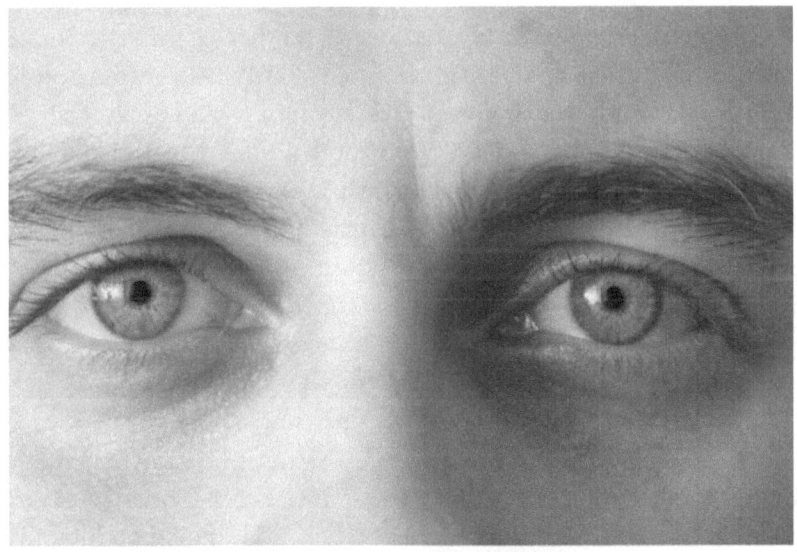

If people realize God's eyes watches them twenty-four seven every day in the week. They will straighten out their way of living. Photo by Kaan Tanriover from FreeImages

The natural man cannot understand how God can look through solid walls and see the activity of millions of people on the Earth at the same time. That is one of the mysteries of God. God's knowledge is far beyond man's knowledge. God knows the number of hairs on your head. He knows us better than we know ourselves! We must Know that God is ALL KNOWING! There is nothing He does not know!

All activity on the Earth is being recorded by God. Every life lived on the Earth is recorded from birth to death. This includes the thoughts, ideas that came to their mind. Man is foolish to live their life as there is no God and when they die, they know nothing. When a person die they go into eternity to be judge on the life they lived here on the Earth. That is why it is so important to be saved, sanctified, and Holy Ghost Filled so it will speak for you when you face eternity. That is more important than education, money, power or material things in this world. Satan will distract people away from Salvation and put their mind on these natural things so a person can die not ready for Heaven. Satan wants people to not be able to enter into the Kingdom of Heaven.

That is why Satan encourages clergies to teach doctrines unto the people to claim Jesus as their Savior but still hold on to sin believing Jesus is going to cover them in their sin. God sent His only begotten Son Jesus into the world to forgive people of their sins. Jesus blood will wash them taking out the old inherited sin from the Fall of Adam. Jesus will take that old sinful nature out and place in you a brand-new nature. The new nature is the nature of God which is called born again. All are these are mysteries how Jesus can take out the old sinful nature out of a person. **I John 3:5-6** *And ye know that he was manifested to take away our sins; and in him is no sin. Whosoever abideth in him sinneth not: whosoever sinneth hath not seen him, neither known him.*

My question is if Jesus take away your sin what desire do you have to commit sin? So, when you have Christians who confess Jesus and still sin. Jesus has not taken away their sins. Every Christian needs to know that! Jesus' blood sanctifies every true Child of God taking out the desire of sin. Once that old sinful nature comes out, they are born again. The blood of Jesus signs their name on Lamb's Book of Life. You see in order for your name to be written in the Lamb's Book of Life you must be Holy, pure, clean, perfect. All those words are synonyms. It is Satan who trick Christians who claim Holiness but shy away from Perfect! You can't be one without the other! One time I was trying to explain that to one person so he could understand. You see Satan will play mind games with Christians over certain words. I understand many Christians shy away from what Jesus said in **St. Matthew 5:48** *Be ye therefore perfect, even as your Father which is in heaven is perfect.* I want you to know it is Satan who want Christians to feel they cannot be perfect like Jesus says so they can enter into Hell Fire. The man I was talking to would go along with Holiness; will shy away from being perfect. I told him Perfect and Holiness means the same thing. It cause him to think. I am asking how can you be Holy like the Bible say and not be perfect? Christians need to wake up! Don't let word terminology confuse you! Perfect and Holiness are synonyms. Synonyms are words that mean the same thing; are spelled differently. All imperfect Christians will go with Satan home into the Fire! Imperfect Christian is another name for sinner!

It is a mystery to the world, how Jesus can take sin out of a person which will make them a brand new person. Apostle Paul says in **II Corinthians 5:17** *Therefore if any man be in Christ, he is a new creature: old things are passed away; behold, all things are become new.* My question is if Jesus makes your life brand new and old things are passed away. How is it that Christians can confess Jesus and still sin with the old things? Are they in violation of **II Corinthians 5:17**? It is something to think about. Jesus comes to save us from our sin and takes sin out of us! God wants all His children to live a change life. Live a life with victory over sin every day! If a person confess Jesus and their life has not changed they are NOT saved!

Some Christians want to use repentance as an excuse to commit sin. God is tired of people repenting all the time! **Jeremiah 15:6** Thou hast forsaken me, saith the LORD, thou art gone backward: therefore will I stretch out my hand against thee, and destroy thee; I am weary with repenting. God wants all His children to REPENT and TURN from their sins! Live a life with victory over sin not sinning anymore. God is very displeased when Christians forsake Him going backward into sin! They repent and keep on sinning. That is NOT good. Time to move on from repentance! **Hebrews 6:1-6** *Therefore leaving the principles of the doctrine of Christ, let us go on unto perfection; not laying again the foundation of repentance from dead works, and of faith toward God, Of the doctrine of baptisms, and of laying on of hands, and of resurrection of the dead, and of eternal judgment.*

And this will we do, if God permit.

For it is impossible for those who were once enlightened, and have tasted of the heavenly gift, and were made partakers of the Holy Ghost,

And have tasted the good word of God, and the powers of the world to come,

If they shall fall away, to renew them again unto repentance; seeing they crucify to themselves the Son of God afresh and put him to an open shame.

God is very displeased at Christians Crucifying the Lord Jesus afresh putting Him to open shame because they keep on sinning and repenting. God wants people to STOP sinning! Jesus told the woman taken in adultery in **St. John 8: 10-11** *When Jesus had lifted up himself, and saw none but the woman, he said unto her, Woman, where are those thine accusers? hath no man condemned thee? She said, No man, Lord. And Jesus said unto her, neither do I condemn thee: go, and sin no more.*

God wants people to stop sinning! Not just slow down but STOP! Jesus said in **St. Luke 15:17** *I say unto you that likewise more joy shall be in Heaven over one sinner that repenteth, than over ninety and nine just persons who need no repentance.* It did not say repent every day like so many Christians do! Another fact is the Holy Ghost dwells in a pure, clean, perfect heart. How can you mix the Holy Ghost in your heart with sin? **St. John 16:13** *Howbeit when he, the Spirit of truth, is come, he will guide you into all truth: for he shall not speak of himself; but whatsoever he shall hear, that shall he speak: and he will shew you things to come.* How can a person have the Holy Spirit and go into sin? There is no need to look at King David because doing his lifetime on Earth King David did not have the Holy Ghost dwelling in him. It come upon him and that is all. The Holy Ghost dwell in the Ark of Covenant. King Solomon said **Ecclesiastes 7:20** *For there is not a just man upon earth, that doeth good, and sinneth not.* Nobody could enter Heaven living like that!

Jesus come to put things on a better promise! *Abraham, Isaac, Jacob, Joseph, Moses, King David, Solomon, Jeremiah, Isaiah* and the prophets had to wait for Jesus to come. Jesus preached to all of them in *paradise* in the grave. Those who believed on Jesus got saved and went to Heaven. The Gospel is preached to the whole world now because there is no repentance beyond the grave! God give people a lifetime to get their soul right before God. Doing that lifetime people can do whatever they like.

They can live like a heathen, worship Islam or false idols, attend false churches, practice witchcraft, or do whatever. When they die, if they don't have Jesus and the Holy Ghost, they cannot enter the beautiful City of Heaven. God give everyone a choice to make. The choices are Heaven or Hell. The way to Heaven is holiness through Jesus Christ and the way to Hell is everything else!

People will say God is love. I agree God is love. The question is How much do you love God? If you love Jesus you will keep his commandments. **St John 14:15** God wants all His children to live right and walk every day in Holiness. Salvation of God through Jesus Christ is a mystery to the world. People feel they can serve God their own way. Others feel they cannot become holy or perfect until they enter eternity. What they fell to realize is to be perfect in eternity we MUST be holy or perfect in our soul now in this life! Look at Jesus how He lived holy in this world. If Jesus lived holy in this sinful world, so can we if we get Him on the inside. As the Scripture says in **I John 4:17** *Herein is our love made perfect, that we may have boldness in the Day of Judgment; because as He is, so are we in this world.* We are to be like Jesus in this world. Let Jesus reign in our mortal body.

God is NOT like man! Once a person breathes out and go into eternity all these natural things does not matter. What is very important is the Blood of Jesus and the Holy Ghost with Fire. People needs to know that. God's knowledge is far beyond man! There is no death in God for He is eternal. I am going to talk next about the eternity of God.

CHAPTER 7

Eternity of God

Man's knowledge is limited that is why all they talk about is birth and death. They feel death is the end of all life. They are right for they see it no more here on the Earth. What man fail to understand life goes on and live beyond this world. The breath of all life comes from God and returns back to God. This means all life from animals, plants, all humans saints or sinners when they departs this planet the breath of life goes back to God. Everyone MUST understand the law of death is only permitted by God to put an END to sin here on the Earth. Death was NOT part of God's original plan. There is no death in God. God is everlasting life! All life returns to God the Creator of all life!

God in His magnificent wisdom made man above all of His creations. He gave man a soul. The soul is the real part of a human. The soul is the one that can move the body. The soul has all five senses to hear, see, taste, touch and smell. This is in addition to the natural body with the breath of life which can also hear, see, taste, touch and smell. Human beings unlike animals can reason and judge because of the breath of life. Unlike animals, when man dies their soul continues to live with those five senses throughout eternity. All those graveyards, cemeteries where people go and mourn over their love ones, the person is NOT what you call dead knowing nothing! They are ALIVE living somewhere!

They are either in Heaven with Jesus or down in Hell Fire with Satan and the demons. Graveyards and cemeteries are ONLY reminders that these people use to live here on the Earth. It shows respect that man is God's Creation. So, to place the body in the Earth show respect to God's Word. The natural body come from the Earth and it returns back to the Earth. **Genesis 3:19**

> *In the sweat of thy face shalt thou eat bread till thou return unto the ground, for out of it wast thou taken; for dust thou art, and unto dust shalt thou return.*

What is wicked in the eyes of God when the world takes and deliberately cremate a human body. I understand it is a modern way of burial and many people are doing it! There are even some Christians who have done it; does not make it right! It is wicked and show disrespect unto God that you are a human in the image of God! It is Satan who hates man and wants you to destroy yourself! Satan will have people burn the body up in fire because he hates man! He wants to burn your soul in Hell Fire! People who choose cremation shows disrespect and no love for God and for themselves. They are telling God, *"I don't mind spending eternity in the fires of Hell."* Cremation of the human body is in connection with witchcraft and demon worship! Natives practice such rituals in their native countries. They burn human beings in so call sacrifices. This is wicked before God. I recommend all Saints of God should have no part with such practices. If someone accidently be burned up in a house, car fire or bomb explosion. Those are NOT counted against you! What displeases God is when people deliberately burn themselves up! That is what I am talking about. The world is wicked and they don't care what happens to their natural body. Although for a true child of God the death of a Saint is precious in the sight of God Psalm 116:15. A Saint of God should be concerned about their natural body which is the temple of the Holy Ghost.

A true Saint who is saved, sanctified through the blood of Jesus, Baptized and Filled with the Holy Ghost and Fire. The Heavenly Gates swings open and Jesus be standing in the distance next to the Almighty waiting for you to come in. That will be a shouting, dancing speaking in tongue Holy Ghost time! I want to be like Elijah flying on the chariot of Fire speaking in tongues, praising God shouting Thank you Sweet Jesus as we ride to Heaven! Glory! Glory

I want to be as Elijah flying to Heaven on the Chariot of Horses speaking in Tongue, shouting Thank you sweet Jesus! https://www.maxpixel.net/Force-Monument-Run-Away-Greatness-Horse-London

Everyone MUST know in this life God allow people to live the life they choose. Man can pass laws supporting gay marriage, common law marriage, abortions and laws permitting marriage between man and their pet cat or dog. They can worship idols, false religions, fight in support of Islam and the Koran. They can live as a heathen smoking plants, drinking alcohol and using opioids or drugs. They can get so educated with Bachelor, Masters or doctorate degrees. Sing to draw crowds making people so call happy! When it comes down for them to die. An Almighty God is looking for the Blood of Jesus, Holy Ghost and Fire. **I John 5:6-7**

> *This is he that came by water and blood, even Jesus Christ; not by water only, but by water and blood. And it is the Spirit that beareth witness, because the Spirit is truth. For there are three that bear record in heaven, the Father, the Word, and the Holy Ghost: and these three are one.*

What will you do? Can *Elijah Muhammad* help you? Can the *Virgin Mary* help you? What can *Buddha* do to help you? Can your good deeds on Earth help you? Can church attendance or singing in the Choir or quartets help you? Can your educational degrees or military service help you? You MUST know these religions are just occupying your time while you are breathing here in this world. Once you depart this world they will dump and soon forget about you! *Homosexual, Lesbian* movements, *Jehovah Witness, Muslims* and other cults will forget about the deceased. They have a so call celebration of life for the deceased and parade to the cemetery or cremation ceremony to say their final goodbyes. Then it is Nice knowing you! They will dump you forever! They will concentrate ONLY on living the life here on Earth now! Why waste time dealing with these false movements?

Jesus will **NEVER** do His Children like that! When a true Saint of God departs this world, they are in the loving hands of sweet Jesus! **Psalms 116:15** Precious *in the sight of the Lord is the death of a saint.*

To depart this world as a Saint of God is to enter into eternal life to live with sweet Jesus. The natural body goes to sleep to wait for God to change it to an incorruptible body for the world to come. That is the reason God command to bury the body in the Earth. The soul goes to Heaven to live with sweet Jesus until the Day of Judgement. The world only sees your shell or body calling that you! That is not really you! That is only your shell! A true Saint of God who is sanctified through the blood of Jesus and Baptized and Filled with the Holy Ghost and Fire will be dressed in a glorious white robe representing the life they lived on the Earth as a true Saint of God.

The reason I preach so much for people to live right because the life we live on this Earth will testify for you up in Heaven! Satan wants people to live a messed up sinful life abusing the mercy of God through Jesus Christ expecting Jesus to cover their sins are in for a rude awakening! There is no forgiveness for willfully sinning. People know it is wrong to fornicate, commit adultery, lie, steal, curse and do it anyway are willfully sinning. **Hebrews 10:26** For if we sin willfully after that we have received the knowledge of the truth, there remaineth no more sacrifice for sins,

Especially when they have an attitude saying, *"God is a forgiving God!"* They are abusing the Grace of God and crucifying the Lord God afresh which is wicked in the eyes of God! **Hebrews 6:4-6**

> *For it is impossible for those who were once enlightened, and have tasted of the heavenly gift, and were made*

partakers of the Holy Ghost And have tasted the good word of God, and the powers of the world to come, If they shall fall away, to renew them again unto repentance; seeing they crucify to themselves the Son of God afresh, and put him to an open shame

God wants people to stop sinning! God is going to whip those clergies who refuse to tell the people to stop sinning. They are messengers of Satan encouraging the people to remain in sin telling them they will not be free until they enter eternity. That is a lie! The bible says in **Revelation 22:11**

He *that is unjust, let him be unjust still: and he which is filthy, let him be filthy still: and he that is righteous, let him be righteous still: and he that is holy, let him be holy still.*

What time will you have to get ready? Leave those false clergies alone and get save, sanctified and Holy Ghost Filled with Fire while you are in this world so you can be ready when sweet Jesus comes. Only the pure in hearts shall see God. **St. Matthew 5:8 You MUST KNOW you only have one chance, one life to live so choose life to make Heaven.** Don't allow false religions, cults, masonic rituals, witchcraft or anything block you from Jesus Christ. Jesus said in **St. John 14:6** Jesus saith unto him, I am the way, the truth, and the life: no man cometh unto the Father, but by me.

Jesus is the ONLY way to get to Heaven. That is the reason I preach the blood of Jesus to wash you and make you white as snow. Get rid of that sinful nature in this world so you can be ready for Heaven. The Holy Ghost dwells in a clean vessel. The Holy Ghost dwells in no sinner! There are too many hypocrites out there fooling the people claiming they have the Holy Ghost, and they commit sin. How can light and darkness mix? How can sweet water and bitter come out of the same fountain? You cannot mix a true saint of God with sin no matter how you look at it. **James 3:11** *Doth a fountain sends forth at the same place sweet water and bitter?* No true Saint of God will be cursing or using any profanity!

If people curse Satan is in their heart! Weak Christians will look at Peter when he denied Christ. **St Matthew 26:74** Yes, Peter did curse and swore because he was NOT totally delivered. When a Christian is NOT totally delivered, they will curse and swear, fornicate or do whatever sin because that sinful nature is still present in their heart. They DO NOT have the Holy Ghost! They are NOT ready for Heaven.

When Peter got sanctified and Holy Ghost Filled you do not see where he cursed, swore or denied Christ anymore. Jesus will get you ready for Heaven. The Real Holy Ghost will seal you until the **Day of Redemption.** Satan CANNOT break the seal of the Holy Ghost and Fire! Satan CANNOT wade through the blood of Jesus to get to a believer to make them commit sin. If that was possible Satan will be saved himself. That devil will NEVER get save! That is the reason the Apostles lived Holy AFTER they received the power of the Holy Ghost with Fire! They had true Holy Ghost power!

When the blood of Jesus and the power of the Holy Ghost come in you, He will cause you to live free from sin in this sinful world. I understand you have many clergies teaching the people they can have the Holy Ghost and still sin. That is NOT Biblical. That is the reason why I stress KNOW the Bible for yourself! Some clergy uses *Theology* and *Philosophy* to teach weak doctrines mixing living for the Lord with sin deceiving the people. I am a preacher who uses the Bible and give you Scripture! I am a Bible preacher! The Bible is the road map to Heaven. DO NOT trust a clergy who uses Theology or Philosophy to preach. Those are man's ideas, and we cannot go to Heaven on man's ideas. We can only go to Heaven by obeying the Word of God!

Jesus will get in us and give us power to obey the Bible. When people disobey the Bible that means they have the devil in their heart. Jesus come to cast that devil out so He can live in our soul. Jesus changes the actions and attitude of a person. Apostle Paul states in **2 Corinthians 5:17** *Therefore if any man* be *in Christ,* he is *a new creature: old things are passed away; behold, all things are become new.*

Jesus will clean your life inside out take out the old desire of sin and place in you a brand-new nature. The nature of Christ that does NOT want to sin. That is being born again. Old sinful things are gone! Your life is brand new inside out! Glory! The blood of Jesus is very strong! It will take sin out by the root! A person will have NO desire to sin. They will have a desire to please the Lord God in holiness and righteousness ALL the days of their life.

What Satan has cast over the world is a zeal of God where you have Christians confessing Jesus, the Holy Spirit and they sin sometimes too. You have clergy teaching the people you can be saved and fall into sin too. Repentance is the main subject on these Christians' mind. Sin and repent their whole Christian life here on Earth. God is NOT pleased with Christians living a life such as this! God wants twenty-four-hour Christians NOT part-time Christians. Those who will serve Him with ALL their soul, might and strength. They will give NO time to Satan.

Everyone MUST know the life we live here on the Earth will determine where we will spend eternity when we exit this planet. We all are preaching our own funeral as we live each day on the Earth! If you want to see those Heavenly Gates to open and Jesus standing on the right side of the Almighty God for you to come in, then you MUST live right while you live here on Earth! This is contrary to these clergies who teaches the people that Salvation is a gift of Grace! The Bible says **2 CORINTHIANS 5:10**

> *For we must all appear before the judgment seat of Christ, that everyone may receive the things done in his body, according to what he hath done, whether it be good or bad.*

The life we live on this Earth, all we do, say and think will be judged by God. What we repent and correct which is wrong and don't do anymore in this life on Earth is sponged from our record. That is something to dance and shout about! Where Christians get in trouble when they continue to do wrong and repent. Never correcting that wrong in this life. Some False Clergy encourage them saying it will come out when they die. That is a lie from Satan to send many souls into Hell Fire. There is NO repentance beyond the grave. Now in this world is the dressing up room to get right with God!

Once we close our eyes for the last time it will be all over. Nobody can help you! The clergy, police, doctor or nobody can do anything to change your destiny. That is what everyone needs to think about when they waste time in some religion, cult, Masonic Lodge, worshiping some idol or in some witchcraft organization. These activities will occupy your time until the last breath leaves the body. Once the last breath leaves, they dump you like I said earlier! Homosexuality and Lesbianism is the same way! They practice that lifestyle all the way until the last breath exits the body, then they forget about you! I want to ask the question why waste time practicing such religions, cults or Homosexuality acts when it will do you no good when you depart this world?

Some churches, cults, even Homosexuals will shy away when someone is deceased. They comfort themselves in believing the lie the dead know nothing! Others will comfort themselves with maybe God will recognize deathbed confessions. I do NOT recommend deathbed confessions because when a person waits until then they are almost at the gate of eternity. God will give each person PLENTY of time to get themselves right! If they allow Satan to fool them by ignoring God's Word. It is counted against them. Every time when God sends a servant to invite them to church service and they refuse to come, it is counted against them. Each altar call they refuse is counted against them.

If a person throughout life refuses the Call of the Lord! Then when they are about to die and they call on the Lord the bible says this in

Proverbs 1:23-26

Turn you at my reproof: behold, I will pour out my spirit unto you, I will make known my words unto you. ²⁴Because I have called, and ye refused; I have stretched out my hand, and no man regarded; ²⁵But ye have set at nought all my counsel, and would none of my reproof: **I also will laugh at your calamity; I will mock when your fear cometh;**

God does not like it when people ignore His call to repentance! God is not pleased when people ignore His Word and commit the sins of the flesh! Look at all of the many Pentecostal-Holiness churches with only a faithful few people in church. All those empty pews God is not pleased when He sees people who could be in those pews at home watching the football game on television. They are lying out on the beach, in the amusement park. Some people are sitting out in chairs along the streets in neighborhoods just passing time. God is NOT pleased. On the other hand, Satan will fill his churches up with people who will listen to watered down doctrine where people have a zeal or form of godliness.

A zeal of godliness is NOT strong enough to get you into Heaven! Those mega churches loaded with people the clergy only preach sermons that people should be kind one to another, husband and wife get along, live a good moral life. Confess Jesus and the Holy Spirit if you sin such as fornicate or commit adultery repent and it will come out in the wash. In these churches people are big on love saying, *God is love* but the question is HOW MUCH DO YOU LOVE GOD? Their love for God is very low for Jesus says in **St. John 14:15** *If you love me keep my commandments.*

They teach you don't have to keep the commandments this is contrary to what Jesus says. They depend on *Grace* of God to give them an excuse to slip into Heaven like some thief. I warn you to stay away from such doctrines because you cannot get into Heaven being disobedient to the Word of God. God sits in Heaven and looks down on the Earth for His children to walk every day in the Word of God. Be blameless of all the sins of the flesh! The Grace of God is there to take care of small matters in a Saint of God's life such as misunderstandings among church people or sinners. Slackness in doing some business of the Lord for the church. Grace of God will iron out all the wrinkles and blemishes in a Saint of God's life. So, they can be perfect ready for Heaven. Spots will keep anybody completely OUT of Heaven. Spots are sin! Jesus blood like I preach and teach will remove sin out of our lives through Sanctification. The Grace of God is for the small matters such as what the bible calls weights, which will hinder your progress in the Lord. **Hebrews 12:1 It pleases God for all Christians to give up ALL the weights.**

God will whip those clergies who mislead people into believing that God's Grace will cover their sins when they die! Satan uses clergies to mislead people into the fires of Hell telling them they can slip into Heaven with sin in their life! I warn you to STAY AWAY from all those false clergies. Believe what Jesus says in **St. Matthew 5:8** *Bless are the pure in hearts for they shall see God.* Question what are you going to do? Will you follow the ideas of man and play games with your soul living a life enjoying sin saying, "*God is a forgiving God!*" Will you risk living a life in sin and depend on begging God near death door for mercy? How do you know you will have time to repent at death door? Some people die suddenly; they have NO time to pray a deathbed prayer! What are you going to do?

People die at all ages. Jesus warns us to be ready for the hour you think not the Son of man cometh. **St. Matthew 24:44** Again, I warn you no matter how young you are or how old we need to be ready to meet sweet Jesus. We don't know when that time will come when we enter into eternity! Satan will play a trick on many people saying, "*You have plenty of time.*" That is to occupy your time, so you do NOT get ready. Satan knows every time a person enters eternity NOT ready; he is ready to grab that soul to carry it to the fires of Hell! Satan plays games making people feel they are going to Heaven anyhow and knock the door down doing like they want to do. Easy said than done! For the Glory of God will leave any man speechless! **In St John 3:3**

> *Jesus answered and said unto him, Verily, verily, I say unto thee, Except a man be born again, he cannot see the kingdom of God.*

If you cannot see the Kingdom of God my question is how can you get in there? Let us all wake up to the truth! Stop wasting time on false religions, church memberships, living a good moral life thinking that will substitute for the Holiness of God. God clearly stated He is looking for the Spirit, Blood and the Water to agree with the Father, Son and the Holy Ghost in Heaven. **I John 5:6-7** He did NOT say education, good works, singing in quartets & choirs, playing in the band, living a good moral life. Those things alone are NOT enough. Visiting the sick, taking in the stranger, seeing those in prison, clothe the naked, feed the hungry, water to the thirsty are NOT enough without **I John 5:6-7. God wants Holiness to go along with our righteousness!**

I understand there will be some people to argue with me believing they can debate with God over what Jesus said in **St.Matthew 25:31-46.** All those wonderful deeds are good, but God want them done from a pure heart. Just like you want to eat your nice Fried chicken, Fish, Steak Dinner out of a clean plate not a dirty plate!

Would you eat your nice Fried chicken dinner out this plate? What do you think about God receiving good works out of a dirty heart? Photo by <u>Michal Zacharzewski</u> from <u>FreeImages</u>

God desires the same! God despises a person guilty of Adultery, common law marriage, homosexuality, lesbian although they do excellent work in feeding the hungry in third world nations, clothing the naked, giving medical care to the sick, rescuing someone from a burning house, burning car, capture a rapist or potential murderer. We as humans will praise a person for a good work, they done overlooking the way they are living. They will praise the person as a Saint but behind closed doors they are dirty with sin. God is NOT like man. People will judge a person who feed their bellies with food, give them medical care, education etc. as a Saint gone to Heaven to be with God. God looks at what they are doing in the bedroom or in the secret chambers. That is why it is so hard for people to understand the way I preach and teach. They get caught up in these wonderful, good deeds. This blind them from the way the person is truly living. We cannot fool God! God sees the whole picture! He does NOT have tunnel vision like so many people have. God sees everything and does NOT leave out nothing!

Make up in your mind to live right in order to make Heaven your home. You will be ready when sweet Jesus comes. Once the last breath leaves this body your life is sealed, and nothing can change it! While we are in this life, we can make all the changes we can. Know that eternity is NOT like life here on Earth. Eternity is life everlasting and there is no death! There is no death in God! Believe in the Bible and Jesus Christ to prepare to meet the Almighty God!

CHAPTER 8

Two places for a Soul to Go

Everyone MUST understand when a person departs this world there are ONLY two places they can go. Heaven to be with sweet Jesus or Hell Fire to dwell with Satan and the fallen angels until the Day of Judgement. Two doors will appear; which door will open will determine to how you lived here on the Earth. A true Saint who dedicated their life to God forsaking the sins and pleasures of this world. Suffered for Jesus namesake through much persecution and served God in prayer and fasting. They are saved, sanctified through the precious blood of Jesus and Baptized and Filled with the Holy Ghost and Fire. God will examine their life and sees the Spirit, Blood and the Water. He sees Holiness therefore He is well pleased. The Door will open to Heaven and the force seven times the force of Gravity will pull you toward those Heavenly Gates! The other door will remain closed. That will be a wonderful, blessed time! Glory! Flying to Heaven on the Chariots of Fire! Speaking in Tongues! Glory! Praising God! Thank you, sweet Jesus!

On the other hand, for a sinner who dies and God sees sin in their life. The Spirit, blood and Water does not agree. Then the Door to Heaven will be closed shut and the other Door will swing open which leads down the long dark tunnel with a light at the bottom. An Angel dumps the soul down the long dark tunnel. This is after a Voice speaks saying, "*Depart from me I know you not! Ye are cursed into everlasting fire prepared for the devil and his Angels and there you will be until the day of Judgment.*" The Force that pulls the person will be greater than the force of Gravity to draw the person down that tunnel. Falling down that nasty, dirty tunnel full of evil creeping things. The stench is unbearable! The force that pulls the soul down is sin! The evil creeping things reaches out to grab the soul. The Soul lands at the base where demons gather it and put it in chains to carry it to the cells of Hell. That is where eternal punishment will begin suffering for the sins they committed here on Earth. Satan an ugly red Dragon laugh an evil laugh at all the new souls which enter Hell.

Satan who sits on his throne in Hell greets them with an Evil laugh and he says what level of punishment they will suffer. Satan's throne is made of Hot molten rock. His throne is really no throne at all! Each time God's Name is spoken up in Heaven it causes a very Loud Thunder down in Hell and Satan is immediately knocked off his rock Throne and force to bow to the Almighty God. He goes down cussing up a storm! It is impossible for Him to get up until God allows him to get up!

Souls are placed in the holding cells loaded in chains. These chains are red hot with fire! In these cells' demons torment the new souls nonstop! Sticking long sharp red hot needles through their skin. The demons would laugh an evil laugh each time they scream with pain. The more they scream the more they stick the red hot needles! They constantly do this laughing at their screams in pain! Souls cry out asking Satan, "*Why are you doing this to us?*" Satan reply in an evil laugh "*I do it because I hate you! I hate you because you are in the image of God and I hate God!*" People will be suffering and wish to die and cannot. It is impossible to die! Demons try their best to kill the souls saying, "*Why don't you die?*" Throughout Hell demons take red hot knives and cut souls up in pieces and after they finish the soul come back together again. The demon begins the process all over. Saying, "*Why don't you just die?*"

So much agony, pain and misery go on in the Jail cells of Hell. After much time in the Jail cells the demons move the souls to one of the Hot pits where it is thrown in bound in red hot chains. In those Hot pits they are loaded with many, many lost souls crying out in misery. The pits are blazing with Fire and souls trying to crawl out the pits. Once they reach the top a demon with a broken wing comes by and knock them back into the Hot pit of fire. Then they start crawling all over again to the top. It is so sad to see those souls trying to crawl out of that hot pit and soon as they reach the top, those demons who are constantly watching would knock them back down in the hot Fire. When the demons do it, they laugh an evil laugh just like they are playing a game! The game is who will be the first to knock them back into the fire!

Throughout the left leg of Hell, you have souls dressed in hot chains burning in the Fire some are liars, adulteress, fornicators, those who use profanity and swear. Haters of God are burning in the Hot pits throughout the left leg. Those who hate people due to the color of their skin and those who were members of racist hate groups are burning in the fires of Hell. Those who steal, rob, and sexual assault will burn in the hot pits. There is a section in Hell reserved for witchcraft workers, palm readers, sorcerers, magicians and fortune tellers. The workers of all black magic will burn in this section of Hell. They are placed in a boiling liquid Fire Lake. Demons sit around the top of the edge just waiting for them to climb up to the top so they can throw them back in the red hot liquid!

There is another section reserved in Hell for *Homosexuals, Lesbians* and *Transgender* along with witchcraft workers who sold their soul to Satan. Now they are being punished for it in Hell! In these sections' souls are trap in a liquid fire which rage out of red hot pits! There are much moaning and people pleading for Death! They try to die and it is impossible to die! Death flees away! No matter where they turn there is NO cooling spot! NOT even a drop of water! Those who have been married multiple times with many husbands and wives while they all are still alive on Earth shall burn intensely in the Fires of Hell along with those who commit fornication and Adultery.

Pop singers, those who sing songs to worship the flesh causing people to dance in the clubs, wild parties etc. souls are burning in Hell. Each time the world plays their song the Fire burns them more in Hell. Satan will tell the demons to bring them out of the Hot pits to come and see him. Satan will say in an evil way, "*Dance for me!*" The demons will shoot more fire under their feet, so they can dance like they did on Earth. The more they dance the hotter the fire felt under their feet. The Fire will be hurting them so bad and Satan with his demons would laugh! Satan will command those who sing the *Blues, Rock & Roll, Pop Singing, Country Music* sing songs promoting murder, fornication, adultery, raping some lady. "*Bring them to me.*" The demons will drag them out of the Hot pits to Satan who will ask them to sing their song. The more they sing the *Blues* or their *Hip-Hop Pop* Songs and danced the more the demons shoot Hot fire under their feet. Satan will laugh along with the demons as they holler, curse and swear for it is unbearable hot!

This constantly goes on until Satan get mad and start cursing sending them back into the Hot pits! Satan commands the demons bring him those who are Comedians and practice witchcraft. The demons will drag the comedians and witches out and Satan will say, *"Amuse me!"* The comedians will crack their dirty jokes and Satan does not laugh! Neither does the demons laugh! Satan began to curse and speak perverse things! The demons shoot fire under the feet of the comedians and they yelled in pain this amused Satan and the demons. Satan cursed and commands the demons to send them back to the Hot pits. For the Witches Satan is a little more compassion. He commands them to perform their magic. The witches performed their black magic powers and Satan laughed an evil laugh!

Satan tell all the witches, warlocks, sorcerers, fortune tellers saying, *"Your punishment will not be so severe as the others. I will make you keepers of my Fire Hot pits!"* Satan command the demons to place all the witches over the Red Hot Fire Pits. Satan will laugh and tell the demons, *"If you push them in, I will laugh!"* The demons all laugh an evil laugh and drag the witches to the top of the Red Hot fire pits. They play a game who can get upset with the witches to throw them into the Fire Pit.

Demons throughout hell will mock the people on Earth dancing in the clubs. Demons will mock those guilty of drinking *alcohol, whiskey, wine* and *beer.* Those who suffer in the Fires of Hell, demons will be there to remind them of their sins. Demons will mock them smoking *cigarettes, pipes, chewing tobacco* and *dipping snuff.* Demons will mock them walking drunk in the street. Every soul who is burning in Hell will know why they are there! Demons will mock those who curse and use profanity! Demons constantly speaking profanity and swearing! Demons will torment the *Homosexuals, Lesbians, transgenders* by taking red hot sharp knives cutting them into pieces. They will be yelling in pain. Once they finish cutting them up. They come back together again. The demons will say, *"Why don't you just die!"* They began to cut them all over again.

They constantly do that over and over again. Satan encourages the law of man to create laws to encourage people to live-in so-called peace a life in abomination unto God as a *Homosexual, Lesbian or Transgender.* Satan encourages man to create laws to make it comfortable for people to have same-sex marriage. Let them make laws to make it comfortable for a woman to have an abortion. People do these things blinded by Satan believing the lie it is alright. The reason is they do not see the Invisible God. They do not believe the written Bible as the true Word of God. Satan has buried them in a lie God made them that way. They were born a *Homosexual* or *Lesbian.*

Some will be so deep in the lie, that they will claim Jesus saved them as a homosexual or Lesbian. Satan will have them believe that lie until they depart this world. Once they depart this world then Satan will be eager for them to come down there to where he is! Satan will take all the Homosexuals, lesbians and transgender moving them from the jail cells to place them to a big lake side pit of Fire and the demons will throw all them in a pile like Crabs on red hot sulfur coals! The demons will guard the lake size pit waiting for one to climb to the top. Once they make it to the top, they knock them back in laughing their evil laugh.

Child molesters and rapist will have their place suffering in the hot pits nearby. A place in Hell is reserved for Clergy who lied to the people luring them into the Fires of Hell. They taught doctrines Satan authorize such as saying Jesus loves them and Grace cover their sins. They can sin as much as they want if you confess Christ Jesus blood will cover them. Clergy shall burn in Hell who make merchandise out of the people robbing them of their money. They live in fine Houses with swimming pool in the back. They have Maga churches allowing people to live a life in sin not telling them the whole Truth of the Word of God. Some clergies are child molesters caught having sexual relations with the church secretary. These Clergies enjoying living in prosperity in this world and now suffering for their sins in everlasting Fires of Hell. They had their so-called heaven in the life they lived in this world.

The Right leg of Hell are reserve for those who are master murders, master thieves, those who commit suicide. Suicide is a sin there is no forgiveness because how can you ask God for forgiveness when you are already dead? Asking God to forgive you before you do it DOES NOT count! Repentance is Lord forgive me I will not do it anymore! God wants people to STOP sinning! In that section of Hell, you have souls who were on a mission from Satan while on Earth to take out many people in a mass bombing blowing up buildings, bridges, shopping malls, government buildings. Satan says, "*Take out as many people as you can!*" Then Satan will say, "*Kill yourself so you will escape the law of man.*" Satan will not tell you about the horrors of Hell Fire. He will encourage you to come in to the Fire and do it in a slick way by saying, "*You will get rewarded in Heaven with so many virgins!*" Some people will be so foolish to believe that lie!

Satan will encourage people to steal merchandise in every way to fool the technology of man. He teaches people to make counterfeit money to pass the tests man can produce to discover it. Satan organizes crime groups to sell drugs run organize *prostitution rings, pornography industries, gambling clubs* and such evils. These people who run such industries to make a living selling their soul to Satan to do such evils. Operate sex clubs which have naked women and men dancing to entertain people. People operating Drug factories getting people addicted to marijuana in so call products. These things Satan uses to draw people into Hell Fire.

The Right leg of Hell will be reserved for Master-Mind crime bosses who operated mobs and committed multiple murders, terrorist which destroyed the lives of many people. Assassins which commit murder for hire! Those who try their best to outsmart the police. Those who rob multiple banks going on crime sprees which cover multiple jurisdictions. Cruel world leaders who led people into War to promote evil deeds such as false religions, slavery of a certain race of people, to steal another countries resources such as oil, gold, diamonds, silver etc. shall be punished in the Hot pits of Hell. Leaders of Crime gangs which are guilty of so many murders, robberies, prostitution rings have their spot in this section of Hell.

There are demons who mock law-enforcement officials on Earth holding these souls who were famous Criminals on Earth committing multiple crimes trying to bribe lawyers to help them escape the punishment of the law of man. These demons will hold on the chains to lock that soul in their grip. Those souls will just burn in the red hot fires of Hell. There is no relief just fire burning! The demons just hold them there and see that they will suffer! Laughing as they yell out in pain! Those who are guilty of murder for hire will suffer in those hot pits. Demons will use red hot rollers to take the lost souls and pull them through the hot rollers tormenting them. The demons try their best to kill them but they will NOT die! The demons start cursing when the souls come back together again!

There are World leaders, Kings, Emperors, Presidents, Civil Rights leaders and Queens are burning in the Hot Fire Pits of Hell reason sin is present! Demons running around making their lives as miserable as they can! The demon possessed individuals on Earth who died are placed in boiling Fire liquid pits! Demons running around all throughout Hell yelling, "*I hate you! I hate you! I hate you!*"

Satan himself sitting on his rock molten throne says, "*I hate you all! I hate you! I want you to die! Die! Die!*" He speaks blasphemy and terrible curse words! Satan is a wicked red dragon with several heads. *Judas Iscariot* who betrayed Jesus and hung himself is trapped in his mouth. Satan looks around Hell and laugh at all the cruel jokes the demons play on the lost souls. The lost souls cry out all throughout Hell worshipping Satan and begging for a drop of water. The demons laugh and create a mirage of a cold lake of water in the hot pits. Thirsty, parched souls run to the mirage and when they get close it disappears into more red hot fire! Satan laughs when the demons create those cold-water mirages and the lost souls falls for it. Demons will lure the lost souls to a swimming pool size cold water mirage. Once the souls jump into it becomes a red hot fire pit. The demons laugh, laugh, laugh!

You may feel all of this is so cruel. Question why do people ignore the Word of God warning people to repent of their sins? Why do people live their life doing the very things God command us NOT to do? People are asked to please give your heart to Jesus. Stop your sinning and they look at the people just like they are insane. Satan has cast a blindfold over the world believing the lie that Hell Fire does NOT exist! That is a cruel joke! They say the church people is trying to scare you! My Question is who will you trust man who tell you Hell Fire is not real to make your life so call easy here on Earth so when you die and face Hell Fire for real it will be too late? Will you believe what Jesus said in **Matthew 13:50** - *And shall cast them into the furnace of fire: there shall be wailing and gnashing of teeth.* **Luke 12:5** - *But I will forewarn you whom ye shall fear: Fear him, which after he hath killed hath power to cast into hell; yea, I say unto you, Fear him.* What about the Rich man and the beggar in St. Luke 16:19-31

There was a certain rich man, which was clothed in purple and fine linen, and fared sumptuously every day:

20 And there was a certain beggar named Lazarus, which was laid at his gate, full of sores,

21 And desiring to be fed with the crumbs which fell from the rich man's table: moreover the dogs came and licked his sores.

22 And it came to pass, that the beggar died, and was carried by the angels into Abraham's bosom: the rich man also died, and was buried;

23 And in hell he lift up his eyes, being in torments, and seeth Abraham afar off, and Lazarus in his bosom.

24 And he cried and said, Father Abraham, have mercy on me, and send Lazarus, that he may dip the tip of his finger in water, and cool my tongue; for I am tormented in this flame.

25 But Abraham said, Son, remember that thou in thy lifetime receivedst thy good things, and likewise Lazarus evil things: but now he is comforted, and thou art tormented.

26 And beside all this, between us and you there is a great gulf fixed: so that they which would pass from hence to you cannot; neither can they pass to us, that [would come] from thence.

27 Then he said, I pray thee therefore, father, that thou wouldest send him to my father's house:

28 For I have five brethren; that he may testify unto them, lest they also come into this place of torment.

29 Abraham saith unto him, They have Moses and the prophets; let them hear them.

> *³⁰ And he said, Nay, father Abraham: but if one went unto them from the dead, they will repent.*
> *³¹ And he said unto him, If they hear not Moses and the prophets, neither will they be persuaded, though one rose from the dead.*

All that truth should make a person believe there is a terrible place call Hell and try their very best to bypass that place! Hell is one way in and NO way out! The only exception is Judgement Day when God shall judge all the nations sentencing the wicked along with Satan and all the fallen angels into the Lake of Fire! ***Revelation 21:8***

> *But the fearful, and unbelieving, and the abominable, and murderers, and whoremongers, and sorcerers, and idolaters, and all liars, shall have their part in the lake which burneth with fire and brimstone: which is the second death.*

So many sinners and lukewarm Christians will try their best to push their love ones and friends into Heaven ignoring what the Word of God says. They judge the person on their view. WE CANNOT GO TO HEAVEN ON OUR VIEWS! People needs to know that! We MUST go through the Word of God! Jesus is our only way to Heaven. How an Almighty God looks at the souls in Hell. He can see the future if they were given a second chance, they would go right back into sin again. That is the reason why it is impossible to fool an Almighty God. So all the mourning, crying, yelling, praying that goes on in Hell is because the Fire is unbearably hot! They want to come out! But to stop their devilish ways NO! Some may say they will stop but God can see through their plea that it is a lie! If given the opportunity they would go right back into that sinful world again. Prayers to Jesus and pleas for mercy from the lost souls in Hell are ignored by God! The demons cry out saying, *"He can't help you now!"*

People MUST realize God is NOT like man! He can see the future where we cannot. People who made it into Heaven are there because God can see through the future if they lived, they would live Holy, free from sin in this sinful world. Unlike what some false clergy and teachers say we get what we don't deserve. Everyone in Heaven is there because they are worthy to be there! God looks at all of our lives and He sees how we live. That is why I cannot stress it enough how it is so important to live Holy in the presence of the Lord. If we love the Lord God, we will keep His commandments through Jesus Christ our Lord and Savior!

I understand it is hard to accept our love one, close friend, co-worker, etc. is gone to Hell, but we cannot throw out this Bible just to satisfy our selfish desires. Some people will say, "*Well we don't know what they told the Lord before they died.*" I want to know how can you treat a loving God like that? Ignore His calls to repentance throughout life, because you are enjoying sin! Then when your so call days of pleasure ends; you are facing death. You don't want to go to Hell, so you are going to pray so God can take you into Heaven. Do you really believe that is going to work? I am serving God, because I hate sin! I love a world that knows no sin! I enjoy doing what is right all the time. I don't want to go to Hell. God wants those to show they love Him by turning against all sin while living in THIS life! Live everyday walking in the Word of God.

God is a jealous God! He wants people to serve Him with their whole heart! That means give NO time to Satan and NONE of his works! That is the reason I preach and teach live free from sin. The Lord Jesus save me when I was thirteen years old forgave me of my sins. The Lord justified me by faith giving me peace in my soul. All my committed sins are forgiven. I prayed and ask the Lord to sanctified me through the blood of Jesus. Jesus truly breathe a life in my soul taking out the very appetite, desire of sin out of my heart. Place in me a brand-new nature of Christ that does not want to sin. Jesus wrote my name in blood in the Lamb's book of Life. I received the Baptism of the Holy Ghost and Fire when I was fourteen years old. Since I got saved so young Jesus kept me clean from going to the clubs. I NEVER tasted alcohol, smoke any plants, got high on drugs, dance at some club or school prom, no girl can testify saying I went to bed with them outside of marriage. I have no child out of wedlock! Yes, I was a virgin when I got married to my wonderful wife Velvet. This is my one and only marriage and God has blessed me with an excellent marriage.

I understand some people may say that testimony is impossible. I want you to know Jesus can save you so you can live right! The problem why so many Christians fall from grace into sin is because that old Adam nature of sin is still present in their heart. As long as the old nature of sin is there, they will sin. Jesus come to take the Old Adam nature out, so you will NOT have a desire to sin! **I John 3:5-6**

> *And ye know that he was manifested to take away our sins; and in him is no sin. Whosoever abideth in him sinneth not: whosoever sinneth hath not seen him, neither known him.*

Sadly, there are many Christians confessing they are saved and even have a nerve to claim the Holy Spirit and still commit sin **I John 3:5-6** condemns them. How can you have the Holy Spirit and sin too? That is impossible! Satan will have Christians living in a fantasy pretending they are saved when in reality they are on their way to Hell because of sin! Just like I said God is a Jealous God. He wants twenty-four-hour Christians NOT just prayer meetings, bible study, Sunday morning Christians. It is sad to die and go to Hell sitting in the church but if people believe they can be saved and sin too that will be their major downfall. God is going to whip those clergies who teaches these devilish doctrines bewitching the people. Hell Fire is going to be waiting for them. I understand these people depend on repentance to give them an alibi to get into Heaven living a shabby life enjoying sin and repenting. That is NOT going to work!

Repentance only works when people ask for forgiveness of their sins and they will NEVER sin anymore! That is the ONLY time. All these Christians playing games sinning and repenting are devilish and not recognized by God. People will tell some young single Christians, "*Why don't you go ahead and sleep with that boy or girl. God is a forgiving God! Everybody is doing it.*" You see how Satan will lure people into sin. Some people will draw young people out the church enticing them to go ahead and move in with that boy or girl because everybody is doing it. "*God will forgive you!*" People are abusing God's wonderful Grace! God is not pleased when people abuse His Grace!

Trying to enjoy sin and run under the umbrella of repentance is NOT the way to serve God! God wants people to come ALL the way OUT of sin. God wants people to serve Him in Holiness. Living a shabby life sinning and repenting playing with Satan will lure you into Hell. There is no need to try to impress Church people, preachers or family. What you need to do is to impress God Almighty for He is the one who judges and His judgement is Holy! Don't take chances with your life. Please make a wise choice and serve the Lord in true Holiness it will be the best decision of your entire life.

CHAPTER 9

Walk Around Heaven All Day

A day in Heaven is a very, very busy day! There are people all over the place! Angels flying around and children running around playing games! So many joyful games be going on until the school bells rings it is time for classes. Saints busy walking around through the beautiful parks, peaceful meadows. There are plenty animals in the parks all very calm and gentle. It is normal to see a *lion, bear, tiger, wolf* to be led by a little child. Saints are riding horses all throughout the parks. There are even flying horses sailing through the air! All giving praises to God Almighty who sits on His magnificent Throne in Heaven. His beautiful face can be seen all over Heaven shinning many times brighter than the Sun. Daytime in Heaven is so beautiful more than the daytime here on Earth. God's magnificent face lights up the sky and there is not a cloud to be seen!

God's magnificent face can be seen all over Heaven causing it to be lit up in daylight. It is a beautiful day in Heaven! https://www.maxpixel.net/

You may ask how do the plants gets water? In Heaven the plants just like the animals have bodies that can go long periods without water unlike the plants and animals here on Earth. All creatures and plants in Heaven have eternal life because there is NO death unlike Earth. Saints are just full of joy, happiness and peace. Love is so abundant in the air!

Saints are Always glad to see their neighbors! They NEVER get tired! Laughter is abundant throughout all of Heaven! Laughter NOT at jokes! Laughter at God's glory, wonderful mysteries and wonders that are hid from this world! Saints are Always desiring to do what is right because that is all they know! All activity goes on and someone sings a melody unto God. The person can come from any of the levels of Heaven. When they sing it can be heard all over Heaven.

Then all the Saints, Angels, children, animals and plants join in the melody, song unto God. They sing a song of worship to the God of the Heaven all in unison. Oh, what a beautiful sound when all their voices blend together in worship to the Almighty. God's smiling face is seen and His glory showers all of Heaven like a gentle rain. Praises and Glory unto God goes on! A gigantic choir appears loaded with many Angels, Saints all dressed in white and they began to sing praises unto God! The Choir can be seen all over Heaven. You see up in Heaven there are no television or radio stations so the Angels entertain all of Heaven between worship services in the Tabernacle not made with hands.

Throughout Heaven Saints are walking around feeling so excited! Their hearts are overjoyed! The Glories of Heaven are so abundant that it captivates their minds! Every Saint will testify without a shadow of a doubt that **Heaven is the Real World.** Look at life here on Earth and how real things are to us. In Heaven it is several times as real. The world paints pictures of Heaven as a cartoon figure or a place among the clouds. Heaven is a real world more than Earth! Saints are living eternal life! Death does NOT even exist!

On Earth the Saints see people living in clay bodies subject to the law of sin and death. We have vital organs A1C levels, heartbeat, blood pressure levels and even breathing rates that has to be in check. People on Earth must eat proper diets, exercise, sleep and have good mental health in order to sustain life here on Earth. No matter how long we live here on the Earth each birthday which comes around we grow older and older. After maturing to an adult our bodies continue to grow older. They grow old obeying God's Word heading back to the Earth from where it came. Hospitals, Doctors and Medical technicians work to keep people bodies alive. When man's knowledge goes to the limit the Angel of death comes in and take the breath of life out. Soul enters into eternity. The clay bodies are sent to the Funeral home to prepare for burial. The clay bodies are place into the ground from where it came. Look at us humans, how some people grieve, cry over the death of their love ones. They are grieving over that body of clay! The real person is gone off into eternity!

People talk about how dead bodies decay and the organs such as the brain, heart, stomach liquify for your bacteria that exist on your large intestines began to eat the body. Poisonous Gases develop which creates horrible odors. These odors are dangerous to life on Earth. That is why we obey God's Word and bury these clay bodies inside the Earth! I understand embalming will slow some of these processes down. Regardless to how much man tries to preserves these bodies over time they will break down returning back to the Earth especially when they are expose to air and extreme temperatures! So we need to look beyond this world and prepare for life in eternity.

In Heaven there is NONE of this! The Saints are living and does not have to worry about a correct blood pressure, sugar level, breathing average etc. Living eternally in a whole new world. They will NEVER get sick, old or suffer any ailments! Saints in Heaven will not even have to go the bathroom like these clay bodies here on Earth. They will be living eternally enjoying life! Their age will be as the age of thirty-three years old. They will NOT get no older. They will be thirty-three years old for eternity.

Walking around Heaven you will see Saints decorating their houses on all levels. Saints are laughing, socializing and having a great time! So much conversation going on talking about the wonderful things of God. Jesus will appear all around Heaven. His appearance will make an already joyous day more joyous! Saints are busy doing good. There is NEVER a dull moment. Although there are different mansions up in Heaven. There are NO jealousy, envies or greediness! Those spirits ARE NOT allowed in Heaven. No matter how elegant, magnificent a Saint's mansion is all the other Saints are so happy just like the mansion is their own. Even those on the first level who just made it into the Kingdom of Heaven are so happy for the Saints. The reason they are so happy they escaped a terrible, horrible place call Hell. Believe me that is much more than enough to be satisfied you made it into Heaven!

Everyone in Heaven is happy and satisfied! Peace fills the air. No thoughts of evil, mistreatments or bad feelings! There is nothing to worry anyone! Just peace, happiness and joy! All the many activities are under the watchful eye of a loving Father God! God is all knowing He hears everything the Saints says and even knows their thoughts.

Oh, how beautiful Heaven is with all the green grass fields, peaceful valleys and crystal-clear lakes! All the creatures are healthy, strong and ready to be on the move. Children are running around on all levels of Heaven. Heaven is full of children! Children are almost everywhere! Jesus loves all the children and walks around blessing them! I am NOT a racist, but I can say there are many African-Americans, African descent up in Heaven. Other races are abundant in Heaven also such as Caucasians, Japanese, English, French, Italian, Spanish, Eskimos, Indians, Chinese, Koreans, Vietnamese, India, Arabs and some Jews shall all be in Heaven! God loves all the nations of the world. These souls who are in Heaven are those who dedicated their life to Jesus while on Earth. Some believed on Jesus in secret fearing Governments who enforce the false religions of Islam, Buddhism, Hindu, Catholic etc. would kill them! Jews are in Heaven who believed on Jesus as being the True Son of God! All nations shall be represented in Heaven. Everyone who are in Heaven will believe on Jesus as being their Lord and Savior. Jesus is the ONLY way to Heaven. Jesus is the ONLY way to the True Almighty God of the Heaven!

Up in Heaven all the Saints will cry HOLY! HOLY! HOLY! Unto Lord God Almighty and the Lamb of God Jesus Christ. Let me clear this issue up, with many church people on Earth. I understand there are a group of believers who recognize Jesus only as Savior and God. The Lord God command me NOT to argue with these believers because they are right into believing Jesus is the only way to Heaven. They are right into living Holy unto God each day on Earth. God said, "*When they reach Heaven, I will straighten them out!*" God already knows we on Earth has NOT seen the Godhead. Why argue, debate over it? The most important thing is to live holy and get to Heaven. Get rid of sin is the most important thing! Believing whether the Godhead is just Jesus or The Father, the Son and the Holy Ghost is NOT Salvation! Believing on the Only begotten Son of God Lord Jesus is Salvation! The Almighty God already knows once a child of God comes home; they will see the Godhead as it is! That will settle the discussion forever!

I understand there are some *Jesus only* believers who will attack those who believe in the Father the Son and the Holy Ghost accusing them of three gods. That is human understanding! They are talking from a human point of view with NO revelations from God. I say again there is no need to argue, debate over the Godhead. Just live Holy and get to Heaven. God did not want His children to make His Godhead a doctrine. Although, there are some who will still insist through their ignorance! I say do not waste time arguing with these believers because it is to no avail. I am NOT going to call my sweet Jesus a liar when He clearly told us He has a Father up in Heaven. **ST. John 5:17** But Jesus answered them, "*My Father worketh hitherto, and I work.*" Also when Jesus was praying who was He praying to? He was praying to His Father in Heaven. It is foolish to say He was talking to himself! The Bible says when Jesus ascended back up into Heaven he sits at the right hand of

God. It did NOT say He sat on His Throne and became God! **ST Mark 16:19** *"So then after the Lord had spoken unto them, he was received up into heaven, and sat on the right hand of God."* In Heaven that matter will no longer be an issue because everyone will be in agreement on the one True God and Jesus Christ the Spotless Lamb of God. The Holy Ghost which sails all over Heaven! Glory to God! I am now going to take a look at the Godhead in the next Chapter.

CHAPTER 10

The GodHead

In Heaven everyone is so fascinated over the Godhead and His magnificent beauty. Its colors are gorgeous more beautiful than any Christmas tree lights on Earth! The Bright colors and its beauty will automatically captivate your eyes to look at the glory of God! God the Father sits on His glorious throne made of pure gold. Precious stones, gems decorate the throne. Many diamonds, jasper, emerald and pearls! God's Throne is so beautiful that it would shock this world until it would be speechless! The Glory of God is around the Throne. God is the Great Creator. Just like I said before the origin of all things begins here. Time- It was created by God. People MUST know in eternity there is no such thing as a yesterday and tomorrow! God ALWAYS exists in the NOW! When God creates time, He sets a today, yesterday and tomorrow. Time exists on the Earth and God give man knowledge to use the rotation and revolution of the Earth around the Sun along with the moon cycles to measure time in days, weeks, months and years. In Heaven the saints ALWAYS live in the present.

God has every soul record of life from the day of conception in the womb until the day they depart Earth. Every thought, action good or bad is recorded in the God's magnificent book of time! Everyone MUST know God is all knowing. God's knowledge is far greater than any genius we have on the Earth. Man's genius is only a drop in the bucket compared to God's unlimited genius! The Origin of all knowledge comes from the Great Creator which covers Science, Mathematics, Physics, Astronomy and Astrology comes from Him. God is the one who can take atoms, molecules as man called them and build a whole Universe of Planets, Stars, Comets, Sun and Moon. He sets the planets at the right number of degrees to rotate on its axis. He sets the stars to shine burning off an endless supply of Hydrogen and other gases. That is amazing because with man if we burn a light bulb, heat or drive a vehicle we have to fuel up because if not we will run dry. The light bulb will blow out and needs to be replace. This not the case with God for our Sun burns continuously throughout many generations and so does the Stars until finally God allows one to explode and create more stars!

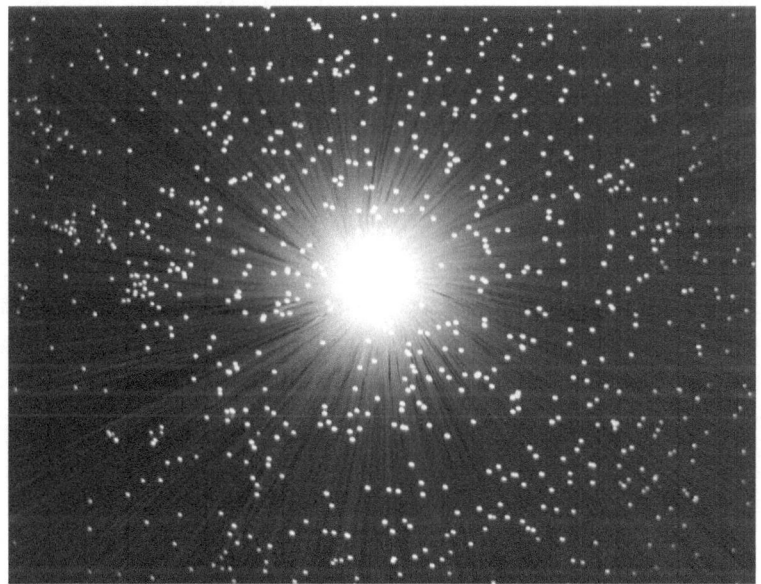

A STAR CAN BURN CONTINOUSLY FOR GENERATIONS
UNTIL GOD ALLOWS IT TO EXPLODE INTO
MORE STARS Photo by Martin K. from FreeImages

God creates the stars set them in place and calls them by name. Man says the number of stars is infinite but with God He knows everyone by name! God even know the number of hairs on our head. He is the Great Creator. God creates on things creatures on Earth for land, air and sea. God creates the creatures and breathe in them the breath of life. Only God the Father can give life! God uses the dust of the Earth to create bodies for all life on the Earth from plants, animals and even man. One thing in the Creation of man God used his own image. Man is in the image of God our Creator that is a great honor!

What is so different about Man is that God gave man a soul. A soul is the real you! It moves insides the body! The soul can have all five senses which can hear, see, touch, smell and taste. Creatures can also see, hear, touch and smell, but it is mixed in the breath of life which will return back to God the Creator at death. God design animals to have the breath of life to live on the Earth. Plants have life to live on the Earth but plants do not see, hear, taste, touch or smell. Man is above all of God's Creations so Man has a soul! The Soul of a Man is eternal and cannot die! These natural bodies dies because it returns back to the Earth like God the great Creator commanded due to sin! I want to let all know Death is NOT in God's original plan. There is no Death in God! God is a God of the living and NOT of the dead!

Everyone MUST know God is eternal which means there is NO such thing as a beginning or an end! We as humans always thinks something comes from something else. The reason is because we are the creation of God. That is all we know because our knowledge is limited. God Himself is eternal and He exists always in the NOW. God is gigantic and fills the whole Heaven, Earth and Universe! All things we know of starts with God! The only exception is Sin and that started with Satan a fallen angel.

On Earth believers honor the Almighty God with several Hebrew names as follows: **Jehovah** which means the True God for He is the Great I AM! Hebrew name is **Yahweh** means the One True God and besides Him is no other! **Yahweh** means God's name is too holy to pronounce! **Elohim** means God. **El Shaddai** means the Lord God Almighty. **El Elyon** means the Most High God. **Adonai** which means Lord Master. **El Olam** means the Everlasting God. All of these are adjectives describing God. His great name is hidden from this world. God loves Holiness and He will NOT allow His name to be spoken through these lips who once knew sin. Only the Saints in Heaven along with the Angels knows His name! We only know God through the Holy Ghost and His only begotten Son the Lord Jesus. I will talk about them later. Worshippers honor His mighty power with **Jehovah- Nissi**. The God that will fight your battle. God knows how to defeat Satan our enemy! He wins a battle every time! Man is no match to the power of God! God is invisible to natural man. It is very hard for man to fight against something they cannot physically see! God uses this as an advantage to defeat man in all his foolish attempts to go against God's Will. No matter how Satan rebel against God. God's mighty power defeats Satan every time!

God is **Jehovah-rophe** A God that heals and make people strong in health. God can heal all manner of sickness and diseases. In God there is no such thing as sickness. God is perfect and every creation He makes up in Heaven is perfect. Sin is the only exception which makes things imperfect. Know God is Almighty and all His creation is Healthy to perfection and not a touch of anything which looks like sickness! Jesus brought this tremendous power to Earth and I will talk about that later. We must know all sickness and diseases come from the result of sin. In Heaven sickness does not even exist.

God is **Jehovah-Raah-** God is a Fantastic Shepherd. He is the Great ONE who can protect ALL His creations! NO power can defeat Him for He is the GREAT I AM. That is the reason when people get save, sanctified & Holy Ghost Filled. God will watch over those soul protecting them from every trick of the devil. On Earth God watches over them protecting them from accidents, sickness, major disasters, those who want to harm them. God does this through His mighty Holy Ghost which I will talk about later

God is **Jehovah-Tisdkenu-** God is full righteousness. Yes! God is good! He is one hundred percent good!

Righteousness all the way around. When people do good deeds it pleases God. Visit the sick, cook food and feed the Hungry, wash clothes for the disable, provide shelter for the homeless, clothe the naked, visit those in prison and give money to support these different ministries all pleases God. Sewing making clothes for the people not overcharging them is righteousness which pleases God.

Greed and the love of money will cause people good deeds to become filthy rags before God when they try to rob people of their hard earn money by overcharging them for their services. God loves when people do their righteous deeds from a pure heart! It pleases God so much when He looks and sees a World full of righteousness! Everybody helping one another! Nobody making fun or trying to hold people down. That is a wonderful world.

Jehovah-Shalom- God of Peace. God will satisfy and make you happy! Enjoy life day by day! Each day give thanks to the Lord for all things! God will make you thankful for all things and stop complaining. Count your blessings and name them one by one. Count your many blessings and see what the Lord has done. Praise Him every time you get a chance. Everyday to the week you praise God. God will shower down blessings unto you! He will satisfy you with good things! No fussing, arguing or debating! Just peace, happiness and joy!

Jehovah-Shammah- God is there. God is everywhere at the same time! He fills the Heaven, Earth and underneath the Earth. He knows everything! It is impossible to hide from Him. Our whole life is naked before God! There is NOTHING He misses! He even knows the thoughts of all these millions of people. That is the reason why God hates liars because it is IMPOSSIBLE to fool Him! God is really amazing! Although down in Hell souls are forever separated from God but God knows what is going on down in Hell. He knows what souls are lost and how they are being punished.

Jehovah-jireh-The Lord will Provide. God will supply your needs. He will not let you go hungry, naked, homeless, thirsty or be sick. He will deliver and give you the victory! When there seems to be no hope God will open up a door of deliverance! He may not come when you want Him; He is an on-time God. God can perform miracles to get your debts paid. God can open doors to put food on your table. Touch people hearts to give you buildings to hold prayer, church services. Doctors can give you a bad report but God will turn things around giving you a victory report blowing the doctors' mind. God is truly amazing!

Jehovah-Mekoddishkem-God who sanctifies. God wants all His children to be Holy for He is Holy! Question how can you enter Heaven being unholy? God loves Holiness. Only Holy eyes shall be worthy to look into His amazing face! God don't want NO sin to come near Him or enter His Kingdom. God wants us to get Holy down here on Earth. Nobody can serve God with sin in their life! Sin has to go! Jesus is the one who will help us get rid of sin once and for all! I will talk about Him later.

Jehovah-Sabaoth-The Lord of Host. He is an Almighty God to be honored! That is in Heaven, on Earth, and underneath the Earth down in Hell.

In Heaven-Angels worship God continually with songs, music and wonderful words of inspiration! Beautiful songs are sung in Heaven. The music honors His great glory, majesty and amazing power! He is the mighty Lord of Host. Saints continually sing praises to the Almighty all throughout Heaven! They sing songs, speak wonderful words of inspiration always giving thanks to the Almighty Children sing songs of worship unto the Almighty! Creatures all throughout Heaven bow in worship to the Lord of Host! The Almighty True God.

On Earth- Saints honor the Lord God of Host through worship and praise! Live a life walking every day in the Fear of the Lord in Holiness keeping God's commandments.

Down in Hell- Satan and the demons tremble in great fear each time God's Holy name is called up in Heaven. The great power of His Holy Name reaches the depths of Hell knocking Satan off his throne forcing him to bow in submission! The Thunder is so great and loud throughout Hell, that all the thousands and thousands of demons tremble in great fear. All are forced to bow to the Almighty Lord of Host up in Heaven. Satan and the demons are cursing up a storm, but they are bowing in submission!

God is the ONE true God and there is no other besides Him! Everyone should know that!

The Son Jesus is the only begotten Son of God. In the beginning in the bosom of His Father! Jesus came out from God as His Word! When the Almighty spoke His Word, Jesus done the work. In fact, Jesus is the one who actually created ALL of God's creations. Jesus in communication with His Father set all the stars in place calling each of them by name. He sets the Sun, planets all in place at the right-angle degrees to rotate on its axis. Set all the planets to revolve around the Sun continually without bumping into each other. Jesus is the one who created the creatures on Earth and even formed man out of the dust of the Earth. His Father breathe in them the breath of life so they can live. Jesus works close with His Father and agree with Him on everything. That is why He says that me and my Father are one!

Jesus is as one brought up with the Father even before the world he was there. God Almighty enjoys communication so His Son is His daily delight! **Proverbs 8:29-31**

> *When he gave to the sea his decree, that the waters should not pass his commandment: when he appointed the foundations of the earth:*
> *Then I was by him, as one brought up with him: and I was daily his delight, rejoicing always before him;*
> *Rejoicing in the habitable part of his earth; and my delights were with the sons of men.*

Jesus appeared all through the Old Testament The **Creation of Adam** Jesus was there. **Genesis 1:26** And God said,

> *Let us make man in our image, after our likeness: and let them have dominion over the fish of the sea, and over the fowl of the air, and over the cattle, and over all the earth, and over every creeping thing that creepeth upon the earth.*

The Towel of Babel confusing the languages of the people causing Nations to come forth. **Genesis11:7**

> *Go to, let us go down, and there confound their language, that they may not understand one another's speech.*

Joshua saw him at Jericho Joshua 5: 13-14

> *And it came to pass, when Joshua was by Jericho, that he lifted up his eyes and looked, and, behold, there stood a man over against him with his sword drawn in his hand: and Joshua went unto him, and said unto him, Art thou for us, or for our adversaries?*
> *And he said, Nay; but as captain of the host of the LORD am I now come. And Joshua fell on his face to the*

earth, and did worship, and said unto him, What saith my Lord unto his servant?

Jesus was in the Fire with the **Three Hebrew Boys Daniel 3:24-25**

Then Nebuchadnezzar the king was astonished, and rose up in haste, and spake, and said unto his counsellors, Did not we cast three men bound into the midst of the fire? They answered and said unto the king, True, O king

He answered and said, Lo, I see four men loose, walking in the midst of the fire, and they have no hurt; and the form of the fourth is like the Son of God

Names and Titles of Jesus:

1. **Almighty One** – *"…who is and who was and who is to come, the Almighty." Rev. 1:8*
2. **Alpha and Omega** – *"I am the Alpha and the Omega, the First and the Last, the Beginning and the End." Rev. 22:13*
3. **Advocate** – *"My dear children, I write this to you so that you will not sin. But if anybody does sin, we have an advocate with the Father--Jesus Christ, the Righteous One." 1 John 2:1*
4. **Author and Perfecter of Our Faith** – *"Fixing our eyes on Jesus, the author and perfecter of faith, who for the joy set before Him endured the cross, despising the shame, and has sat down at the right hand of the throne of God." Heb. 12:2*
5. **Authority** – *"Jesus said, 'All authority in heaven and on earth has been given to me." Matt. 28:18*
6. **Bread of Life** – *"Then Jesus declared, 'I am the bread of life. Whoever comes to me will never go hungry, and whoever believes in me will never be thirsty.'" John 6:35*
7. **Beloved Son of God** – *"And behold, a voice from heaven said, "This is my beloved Son, with whom I am well pleased." Matt. 3:17*
8. **Bridegroom** – *"And Jesus said to them, "Can the wedding guests mourn as long as the bridegroom is with them? The days will come*

when the bridegroom is taken away from them, and then they will fast." Matt. 9:15

9. **Chief Cornerstone** – *"The stone which the builders rejected has become the chief corner stone." Ps. 118:22*

10. **Deliverer** – *"And to wait for his Son from heaven, whom he raised from the dead, Jesus who delivers us from the wrath to come." 1 Thess.1:10*

11. **Faithful and True** – *"I saw heaven standing open and there before me was a white horse, whose rider is called Faithful and True. With justice he judges and wages war." Rev.19:11*

12. **Good Shepherd** - *"I am the good shepherd. The good shepherd lays down his life for the sheep." John 10:11*

13. **Great High Priest** – *"Therefore, since we have a great high priest who has passed through the heavens, Jesus the Son of God, let us hold fast our confession." Heb. 4:14*

14. **Head of the Church** – *"And he put all things under his feet and gave him as head over all things to the church." Eph. 1:22*

15. **Holy Servant** – *"…and grant that Your bond-servants may speak Your word with all confidence, while You extend Your hand to heal, and signs and wonders take place through the name of Your holy servant Jesus." Acts 4:29-30*

16. **I Am** – *"Jesus said to them, "Truly, truly, I say to you, before Abraham was, I am." John 8:58*

17. **Immanuel** – *"…She will give birth to a son and will call him Immanuel, which means 'God with us.'" Is. 7:14*

18. **Indescribable Gift** – *"Thanks be to God for His indescribable gift." 2 Cor. 9:15*

19. **Judge** – *"…he is the one whom God appointed as judge of the living and the dead." Acts 10:42*

20. **King of Kings** – *"These will wage war against the Lamb, and the Lamb will overcome them, because He is Lord of lords and King of kings, and those who are with Him are the called and chosen and faithful." Rev. 17:14*

21. **Lamb of God** – *"The next day John saw Jesus coming toward him and said, "Look, the Lamb of God, who takes away the sin of the world!" John 1:29*

22. **Light of the World** – *"I am the light of the world. Whoever follows me will never walk in darkness, but will have the light of life." John 8:12*

23. **Lion of the Tribe of Judah** – *"Weep no more; behold, the Lion of the tribe of Judah, the Root of David, has conquered, so that he can open the scroll and its seven seals." Rev. 5:5*

24. **Lord of All** – *"For this reason also, God highly exalted Him, and bestowed on Him the name which is above every name, so that at the name of Jesus every knee will bow, of those who are in heaven and on earth and under the earth, and that every tongue will confess that Jesus Christ is Lord, to the glory of God the Father." Phil. 2:9-11*

25. **Mediator** – *"For there is one God, and one mediator between God and men, the man Christ Jesus." 1 Tim. 2:5*

26. **Messiah** – *"We have found the Messiah" (that is, the Christ)." John 1:41*

27. **Mighty One** – *"Then you will know that I, the Lord, am your Savior, your Redeemer, the Mighty One of Jacob." Is. 60:16*

28. **One Who Sets Free** – *"So if the Son sets you free, you will be free indeed." John 8:36*

29. **Our Hope** – *"...Christ Jesus our hope." 1 Tim. 1:1*

30. **Peace** – *"For he himself is our peace, who has made the two groups one and has destroyed the barrier, the dividing wall of hostility," Eph. 2:14*

31. **Prophet** – *"And Jesus said to them, 'A prophet is not without honor, except in his hometown and among his relatives and in his own household." Mark 6:4*

32. **Redeemer** – *"And as for me, I know that my Redeemer lives, and at the last He will take His stand on the earth." Job 19:25*

33. **Risen Lord** – *"...that Christ died for our sins according to the Scriptures, that he was buried, that he was raised on the third day according to the Scriptures." 1 Cor. 15:3-4*

34. **Rock** – *"For they drank from the spiritual Rock that followed them, and the Rock was Christ." 1 Cor. 10:4*

35. **Sacrifice for Our Sins** – *"This is love: not that we loved God, but that he loved us and sent his Son as an atoning sacrifice for our sins." 1 John 4:10*

36. **Savior** – *"For unto you is born this day in the city of David a Savior, who is Christ the Lord." Luke 2:11*

37. **Son of Man** – *"For the Son of Man came to seek and to save the lost.» Luke 19:10*

38. **Son of the Most High** – *"He will be great and will be called the Son of the Most High. The Lord God will give him the throne of his father David." Luke 1:32*

39. **Supreme Creator Over All** – *"By Him all things were created, both in the heavens and on earth, visible and invisible, whether thrones or dominions or rulers or authorities-- all things have been created through Him and for Him. He is before all things, and in Him all things hold together...." Col. 1:16-17*

40. **Resurrection and the Life** – *"Jesus said to her, «I am the resurrection and the life. The one who believes in me will live, even though they die." John 11:25*

41. **The Door** – *"I am the door. If anyone enters by me, he will be saved and will go in and out and find pasture." John 10:9*

42. **The Way** – *"Jesus answered, «I am the way and the truth and the life. No one comes to the Father except through me." John 14:6*

43. **The Word** – *"In the beginning was the Word, and the Word was with God, and the Word was God." John 1:1*

44. **True Vine** - *"I am the true vine, and My Father is the vinedresser." John 15:1*

45. **Truth** – *"And you will know the truth, and the truth will set you free.» John 8:32*

46. **Victorious One** – *"To the one who is victorious, I will give the right to sit with me on my throne, just as I was victorious and sat down with my Father on his throne." Rev. 3:21*

47. **– 50. Wonderful Counselor, Mighty God, Everlasting Father, Prince of Peace** – *"For to us a child is born, to us a son is given, and the government will be on his shoulders. And he will be called Wonderful Counselor, Mighty God, Everlasting Father, Prince of Peace." Is. 9:6*

Jesus is the Great physician to heal ALL manner of sickness and diseases. Doing his ministry on Earth he went about healing the sick, casting out devils and restoring sight to the blind. He was destroying the works of the devil. Jesus did so many wonderful things that there is not enough books to write all the things Jesus done. St John 21:24-25 *This is the disciple who testifieth of these things and wrote these things, and we know that his testimony is true. And there are also many other things which Jesus did, which, if they should be written every one, I suppose that even the world itself could not contain the books that should be written. Amen.* Jesus can work miracles and heal bodies of sickness and diseases today in our generation! God does NOT change!

Jesus sits on the right side of His Father up in Heaven being our High Priest and Intercessor. St. Mark 16:19

> *So then after the Lord had spoken unto them, he was received up into heaven, and sat on the right hand of God.*

I believe what the Bible says. Now the Bible say Jesus went up into Heaven and sit on the right hand of God. It did not say he went into Heaven and sat on His Throne in Heaven and became God. I stress in my book there is no need to fight over the Godhead. God already spoke to me saying, *"I will straighten them out when they enter into Heaven."* God already know the people don't really know, so why waste time debating, arguing over it? The most important thing is to live Holy so you can make it into Heaven.

Ezekiel saw Jesus as a **wheel in the middle of a wheel Ezekiel 1:15-16**

> *As I watched the four creatures, I saw something that looked like a wheel on the ground beside each of the four-faced creatures. This is what the wheels looked like: They were identical wheels, sparkling like diamonds in the sun. It looked like they were wheels within wheels, like a gyroscope.*

Daniel saw **Jesus as a Stone hewn out of a mountain Daniel 2:45**

> *Forasmuch as thou sawest that the stone was cut out of*
> *the mountain without hands, and that it brake in pieces*
> *the iron, the brass, the clay, the silver, and the gold; the*
> *great God hath made known to the king what shall*
> *come to pass hereafter: and the dream is certain, and the*
> *interpretation thereof sure.*

Jesus is the Alpha and Omega the beginning and the end. Time as we know begins and ends with him. What we know as a yesterday, today and tomorrow comes from Jesus. God the Father lives in eternity.

Jesus knows we are human and we think human thoughts. That is why people debate over the Godhead saying Jesus, God the Father and the Holy Ghost are three gods. It takes a Spiritual mind to understand this deep mystery of the Godhead. God has given me these revelations to share with you because I humble myself unto Him.

The Holy Ghost

The Holy Ghost is the third person in the Godhead. That is God's wonderful Spirit which goes out throughout the Universe and into the Earth. The Holy Ghost fills the whole Heaven and Earth. That is why King David wrote where could he flee from His presence? **Psalm 139:7-10**

> *Whither shall I go from thy spirit? or whither*
> *shall I flee from thy presence?*
> *If I ascend up into heaven, thou art there:*
> *if I make my bed in hell, behold, thou art there.*
> *If I take the wings of the morning,*
> *and dwell in the uttermost parts of the sea;*
> *even there shall thy hand lead me,*
> *and thy right hand shall hold me.*

It is impossible to hide from the presence of God. When people try to run from God, they are just wasting time. Jonah learns that when he fell into the belly of a big fish. **Jonah 1-2 Chapters**. Even deep in that belly he was still in the presence of God. The Holy Ghost came in three men and visited Abraham telling him his wife Sarah is going to have a son. **Genesis 18 Chapter** The Holy Ghost spoke to Moses out of the burning bush. **Exodus 3:1-17** The Holy Ghost descended in Fire on Mount Sinai to talk with Moses. **Exodus 19 Chapter** The Holy Ghost and Fire burns. Satan and all the rebelling demons are no match for this tremendous power. The Holy Ghost dwells in the Ark of Covenant to live among Israel because no one was clean enough for the Holy Ghost to live in because of sin. **Exodus 25 Chapter**

The Holy Ghost came on people such as King David when he slew Goliath the Giant. **1 Samuel 17:1-25:7 The Holy Ghost coming on you is NOT like being baptized and Filled with the Holy Ghost**. We humans sometimes get it confused. When the Holy Ghost gets on people, it can get off! This explains how some Christians can dance, shout and even make up a tongue. Then later say, *"Get out my face!"* Some may be using profanity. That is not being a true child of God.

Jesus came to clean us up so we can receive the baptism of the Holy Ghost and Fire in our soul. God loves Holiness so in order for His precious Spirit to dwell in us we MUST be pure on the inside. It is only one way to be pure that is through the blood of Jesus. That is why Sanctification is so important. It is the power of Jesus blood to root out the very desire of sin and place in us a brand-new nature of Christ that does not want to sin. This makes us pure and a candidate to receive the Baptism of the Holy Ghost and Fire. You cannot no matter how hard you try receive the Holy Ghost on top of sin! Jesus is the Only way to God. **St John 14:6** *Jesus saith unto him, I am the way, the truth, and the life: no man cometh unto the Father, but by me.*

The names of the Holy Ghost are:

1. Breath Of The Almighty
   Job 33:4

   Meaning-The Holy Spirit is the life-giving breath of God!

2. Counselor & Comforter
    John 14:16, 26; 15:26 and Romans 8:26

    Meaning- The Holy Spirit is our comforter, our counselor and He gives us strength!

3. Spirit of Counsel
    Isaiah 11:2

    Meaning- The Holy Spirit will counsel us and teach us as we grow in Christ!

4. Eternal Spirit
    Hebrews 9:14

    Meaning-The Holy Spirit is the eternal God!

5. Free Spirit
    Psalm 51:12

    Meaning-The Holy Spirit is a generous and willing spirit!

6. Acts 5:3-4
    Meaning- The Holy Spirit is God as the Third Person of the Trinity!

7. Good Spirit
    Nehemiah 9:20; Psalm 143:10

    Meaning- God's Spirit will teach us and lead us in goodness!

8. Holy Spirit
    Psalm 51:11, Luke 11:13, Ephesians 1:13, 4:30

Meaning-God is the Spirit and He is Holy! He is the Spirit of Holiness.

9. Lord
    2 Corinthians 3:16-17

    Meaning- As the Third Person in the Trinity, the Holy Spirit is recognized and worshiped as the Lord!

10. Power of the Highest
    Luke 1:35

    Meaning- The Spirit of God's Power, He is the greatest power!

11. Spirit of Might
    Isaiah 11:2

    Meaning- He is the Spirit of strength.

12. Spirit of Adoption
    Romans 8:15

    Meaning- By this Spirit we are made heirs of God

13. Spirit of Burning
    Isaiah 4:4

    Meaning- He is the fire of purification!

14. Spirit of Judgment
    Isaiah 4:4, 28:6

    Meaning-The Spirit brings conviction and judgment.
    Spirit of Christ (Jesus Christ)

15. Romans 8:9, 1 Peter 1:11

    Meaning- The Holy Spirit is the Spirit shared between Jesus and God

16. Spirit of Glory
    1 Peter 4:14

    Meaning-The Holy Spirit always gives Glory to God!

17. Spirit of God
    Genesis 1:2, 1 Corinthians 2:11, Job 33:4

    Meaning- The Holy Spirit is the Spirit of the Triune God!

18. Spirit of Yahweh, (Spirit of the Lord Yahweh)
    Isaiah 11:2, Isaiah 61:1

    Meaning- The Spirit has the sacred name for God-Yahweh!

19. Spirit of Grace
    Zechariah 12:10, Hebrews 10:29

    Meaning- He is a Spirit of Grace!

20. Spirit of Knowledge
    Isaiah 11:2

    Meaning-The Holy Spirit has clarity of Mind.

21. Spirit of Truth
    John 14:17, 15:26

    Meaning-The Holy Spirit is about truth not falsehood!

22. Spirit of Life
Romans 8:2

Meaning-The Holy Spirit gives life!

23. Spirit of Understanding
Isaiah 11:2

Meaning-The Holy Spirit is understanding!

24. Spirit of Wisdom
Isaiah 11:2, Ephesians 1:17

Meaning- The Holy Spirit is wise!

25. Spirit of the Living God
2 Corinthians 3:3

Meaning-The Holy Spirit is the Spirit of the One True God who is the God of Life!

26. Spirit of Prophecy
Revelation 19:10

Meaning- The Holy Spirit inspires true prophecy!

27. Spirit of the Father
Matthew 10:20

Meaning- The Holy Spirit is shared between the Father and the Son.

28. Spirit of the Fear of the Lord
Isaiah 11;2

Meaning- The Spirit of the Spirit of reverence toward our God.

29. Spirit of the Lord (God)
    Acts 5:9

    Meaning-The Holy Spirit is the presence of the Lord.

30. Spirit of the Son
    Galatians 4:6

    Meaning-The Holy Spirit shared between the Son and the Father.

These Names of the Holy Ghost explain what the power of the Holy Ghost can do. It is more than a tongue. Speaking in Tongues is one of the evident signs of the Holy Ghost! The Tongues comes out of your belly NOT out of your head. **St. John 7:38** *He that believeth on me, as the scripture hath said, out of his belly shall flow rivers of living water.*

Speak as the Spirit gives utterance! I am a tongue-talking Holy Ghost Filled Preacher! The Holy Ghost comes to empower a child of God to be able to fight Satan and resist the temptation of sin. God wants all His children to live in this world free from sin.

In Heaven the Holy Ghost works mightily in the Saints, Angels, Arc-Angels, children, creatures and even the plants. He causes them to sing praises, dance, shout and worship the Almighty in the beauty of Holiness. The Holy Ghost is God working in all His creations. That is the one true God who sits on His Mighty Throne in Heaven.

I understand the Godhead is a mystery to the human man. That is why you have Christians debating over it trying to prove their point. I stress there is no need arguing over something you have not seen. It is God's wonderful plan to reveal His magnificent Godhead to every believer who enters into the Beautiful Gates of Heaven. Let us work hard to be in that number when the Saints goes marching into those wonderful Gates. I stress over and over to live Holy while in this world!

Without Holiness no man or woman shall see the Lord!

CHAPTER 11

Confusion

God has some wonderful plans for His children and Satan wants many souls miss those beautiful plans. Satan was once in Heaven and he knows how wonderful it is, so he will try to keep us out, because he cannot enter there anymore. So, he has the wicked attitude he cannot enter he don't want us to enter. He plays his evil schemes on the human nature of man. I am going over some of his tricks. One tactic is diverting people attention off of Jesus and working out their soul salvation and focus their attention on money, houses, cars, enjoying the world, living life to the fullest. Some worship the sins of the flesh of fornication and adultery. We living in a sex crazed society!

What you see on Television or hear on the radio are programs, songs talking about the lust of the flesh. People say to a woman, "*You need a man.*" Others say to a boy, "*You need a girl.*" In other words, they promote fornication & common law marriage. You have homosexual and Lesbianism on the rise. Same-sex Marriage society is calling that normal living. People are so hungry for money, gold, diamonds, silver, copper or anything of value. Some people will lie, steal, cheat or gamble to get a dollar. *Casinos,* gambling establishments and games shows such as *The Price Is Right, Let's Make a Deal, Wheel of Fortune* and *Family Feud* are popular among the people. Senior Citizens goes faithfully to the *bingo* games trying to win a prize. All these things are not pleasing unto God!

Satan will try his best to divert people's attention away from Salvation in Jesus to what is going on in this world. Satan uses Education by allowing people to excel in their college degrees. They get doctorate degrees and think they are somebody. A so call big shot in their community with a sad story of how poor they were as a child. Some people will use the *racist* card saying because they were Black it was hard for them when they were a child. I understand it was hard for African-Americans in this country. I suffered much as a Black man in my careers. God is faithful and will bring me out in the right season. Some Christians are so impatient and cannot wait on the Lord.

Satan uses this weakness to force these Christians to take matters in their own hands. Christians will compromise their faith by either telling lies, falsifying documents, gambling, defrauding or doing something evil trying to gain a dollar. Trying to be accepted in society. Look at young people who will do foolish things such as drinking tremendous amounts of alcohol or have sex out of wedlock trying to be accepted in this world. Other young people get drunk off of alcohol and go riding in a car. While drunk driving they hit a tree or another car causing a serious accidental death or serious injury! Parents come running to the Hospital crying and want to see their child who is serious injured, in a coma or even dead. These are the results of sin.

Alcohol related accidents are the results of sin.
Photo by michel collot from FreeImages

One Christian who was a member of a Holiness church told me he was tired of people passing him on side of the road and will not stop to help him because he attended the Sanctified Church. This man wants to be accepted, so he left the Holiness church to go and join up with some other doctrine church which pleases the people. When you truly love the Lord, you will not take down or compromise the Word of God because people treat you wrong. That is the way I live. Since Jesus wonderfully save, sanctified and baptize me with the precious Holy Ghost with Fire the world did not treat me right. I was laughed at, mocked, because I did not live a life in fornication. That is alright, I suffered it out as a humble child of God.

So many young people will be quick to have sex out of wedlock. Others will start living in common law marriage. There are teen pregnancies and the risk of sexuality transmitted diseases because people trying to be accepted. You even have Senior Citizens living in common law marriage. Satan have them in that trap hoping when they die it will carry them to Hell.

How many boys be in the stores with their pants hanging down? Others even have tattoos on their bodies. Young people will try to drink *alcohol*, smoke plants or use *marijuana*, crack or *opioids* trying to be accepted. I made up my mind to follow Jesus regardless how much I get criticize. I am not trying to be accepted in society, but I want to be accepted in that number when the Saints of God goes marching into the Pearly Gates of Heaven. You all must know this world as we know it is only for a season. No matter how long you live *twenty, thirty, forty, fifty, sixty, seventy* or *eighty* more years, it will all come to an abrupt end.

Eternity is what everyone needs to be concerned about. People are constantly departing this planet. They are leaving behind their worldly possessions for someone else to fight over until they die. I stress all Christians do not put your focus on these earthly possessions such as *land, houses, gold, silver, diamonds, money, oil etc.* These only last for a season. Money does answer all things. **Ecclesiastes 10:19 Money cannot buy good health, happiness and eternal life.** There are millionaires who are loaded with money but their health is bad. Some millionaires would be glad to trade their wealth for a season of excellent health! That is the reason I preach and teach Jesus. If you seek Jesus and live holy while in this world you can enjoy riches for eternity in Heaven.

If I had the choice, I rather enjoy my riches throughout eternity with sweet Jesus. Lay your treasures in Heaven where there are no thieves to break through and steal. **St. Matthew 16:19-21**

> *Lay not up for yourselves treasures upon earth, where moth and rust doth corrupt, and where thieves break through and steal:*
> *But lay up for yourselves treasures in heaven, where neither moth nor rust doth corrupt, and where thieves do not break through nor steal:*
> *For where your treasure is, there will your heart be also.*

This is how Satan fool so many Christians by setting their attention on these worldly goods and allowing their soul go lacking in the Spirit. The *Spirit of prosperity* has captivated the minds of many Christians. Satan uses the love of money to lure many souls into the fires of Hell. I advise all Christians to work out your soul salvation and live each day walking in the Word of God. Love the Lord God by serving your Brothers and Sisters in feeding the hungry, visiting the sick, taking in the stranger, water to the thirsty, visiting them in prison and clothe the naked. This along with your holiness, you can be rich in Heaven throughout eternity. Know that it takes Holiness to get your *Crown of Eternal Life*. It takes all your righteous works to get you riches beyond this world to enjoy for eternity.

Saints of God have a hope in Jesus, so they can suffer these years here on the Earth in *poverty, sickness, depression, name calling* and *mockery*. The world has no hope so they struggle to gain this world to enjoy for about sixty years on the Earth. When they closed their eyes for the last time in this world, it is all over! Naked they came into this world and naked they go out! The most important thing is to work out your soul salvation. Prepare your soul for the world to come. Just to enter into Heaven will be worth all the suffering in this world. This includes the name calling, mockery or false accusation. Satan will have people laughing, saying it is all a joke! They will be saying, *"God is not real! Heaven or Hell is not real!"* They will be laughing speaking evil against a God they do not know.

When I was growing up at home, my sanctified Holy Ghost Filled mother would be spending time on her knees praying to sweet Jesus in her room. She would be fasting and going to church while neighbors in the community would be in the backyard at a house sitting at a picnic table drinking cold *Miller High Life* beers. The neighbors would be laughing enjoying themselves doing the summer months. They lived their lives drinking alcohol having a so call good time until they exited this planet.

Celebrating drinking alcohol having a so called good time worshipping Satan. Photo by <u>jim reilly</u> from <u>FreeImages</u>

Satan will hold them in that trap until they breathe the last breath of life out of this world. Once they exit this world and go off into eternity. If they die in their sins, Satan has them in his hands. It is impossible for them to get away. Eternity is a place if a person enter as a sinner will remain a sinner and it is impossible to change. If a person enter eternity save, sanctified through the blood of Jesus and Baptized and Filled with the Holy Ghost /Fire then Jesus will claim that soul. It will be impossible for that soul to get away. My Sanctified, Holy Ghost Filled mother went home to be with sweet Jesus while the other neighbors who preferred to waste time drinking cold beers doing the summer months went off into eternity to where they work to go.

The world is horrified of death and what is beyond. That is the reason they want to concentrate on living in this world now! When a person suddenly departs this planet, they will try to forget them, brushing it off saying the person is dead now! They say this using the *graveyard* or *urn* as evidence. I want to let you know do not allow Satan to capture you into that trap! As we live in this world make sure you work your salvation completely out so you will be ready when sweet Jesus comes.

Satan is determined to keep as many souls as he can out of Heaven. He has many ways to bring confusion into the world to stir people away from a loving God and His plan of Holiness. Tricks such as luring people into *false churches, religions* and *cults.* Satan don't care how many good deeds you do or how many times you were baptize in water in whatever name you please, just as long as you have sin in your life, Satan is satisfied. Others may try to get to righteousness through climbing up in the Masons.

The Masons symbol and all its degrees is not strong
enough to get someone into Heaven. It takes Jesus!

No matter how high you climb up the Masonry, it will not get you free from your sins. Some people get into the Free Masons to do righteous deeds such as building Hospitals for the sick and other good things helping the people. They say they believe in a *Supreme Being* but they operate in secret such as *fun houses* to promote the sins of the flesh such as *Adultery, fornication, homosexuality* which is evil in the eyes of God. Some men who are free mason wives may wonder what goes on in those so call fun houses? That is why secrecy is such an issue!

You can climb up in degrees, *the entered apprentice, fellow craft* and the highest *Masters* but it does not compete with the blood of Jesus. The Free Masons is a Secret society. Again why the secrecy? What are you trying to hide? God has NO secrets! All He does in in the open for ALL to see! That is why I say the Free Masons are of the devil. No true child of God should be involved in such wickedness!

People can dress up in excellent clean clothes and worship idols, sings songs in false religions, go to church on Saturday instead of Sunday. An Idol cannot see, hear or talk why bow and worship something like that? **Satan don't care what you do as long you do not worship Jesus the true way to Heaven!**

Satan will have people worship idols

In fact, Satan don't care what you do as long as you don't get completely free from your sins. **Jesus is the only way to freedom from sin. The Key to making it into Heaven is to give up sin in this life and dedicate your entire life to Jesus**. When Jesus moves in Satan is cast completely out. That is when a person is truly save! Jesus come to set us totally free from sin. There are many Christians out there who confess Christ and still commit sin. They say you have sins of omission and commission. There are clergies out there who say a Christian has sins that you don't know anything about. Listen to how foolish that sounds. God do not have His people in the dark. God will let you know when a person commit sin. I warn all Christians do not allow Satan to hold you in that trap! He doesn't want you to believe you can live in this world free from sin. **Satan knows as long as you claim sin, you have no chance of entering Heaven.** I stress the importance of giving up sin!

You cannot be saved with sin still operating in your life. Don't let Satan hold you in that trap! Repentance is to pray asking God for forgiveness of your sins you will not do it anymore. Once God forgives you of that sin, you are to turn from that sin not to do it anymore in this life. That is true repentance. Time for Christians everywhere to stop playing games straddling the fence! You cannot go to Heaven living an up and down life confessing Christ in church and cursing like the Devil at home!

Time for people to get right with God! Stop playing games with your life! We are only living one time and have one chance. We need to use our time wisely. Get our soul right with God. We don't know when Jesus going to come! **It pays to get ready and stay ready!** Through all the confusion follow Jesus in Holiness, so you can make Heaven your home!

CHAPTER 12

The Marriage of the Lamb

The Marriage of the Lamb of God unto the Church is the most wonderful event which will occur in the New Jerusalem up in Heaven. After the rapture of the Church from Earth and the First Resurrection of all the Saints of God bodies who were asleep inside the Earth. The Almighty God will bring to life these dead bodies turning them into brand new supernatural bodies, just like His only begotten Son the Lord Jesus. All those Saints who have gone to Heaven will receive their brand-new glorified body. Those Saints alive on Earth will be changed faster than you can blink your eye into a brand-new glorified body. The Church will gather up together to take their flight into Heaven.

Once in Heaven Jesus shall present them as a chaste virgin to His Father who will judge their life. When He sees no sin, He will say in a soft voice, "*Well done thou good and Faithful servant. You have been faithful over a few things. I shall make you rulers over many! Enter the joys of my Kingdom.*" All the Saints will be place in their assigned areas in Heaven with their Crown of life! They all will be getting ready for the Marriage of the Lamb to the church.

A. Marriage

After God destroys the wicked and take Satan and all his demons and locked them away in the bottomless pit. The Earth will be cleansed and it is prepared for the Millennium of Jesus and the Church reign for a thousand years. I called this the Honeymoon phase of the church. Up in Heaven there is preparation for a big Wedding celebration. The Saints goes into the Tabernacle not made with hands into the large room furnished with fabulous tables. Angels are busy fixing the tables filling it with many good things for the Saints brand new supernatural bodies. Food such as honey, fruit, vegetables, nuts and milk are served. This food tastes some kind of good! Saints are sitting at the tables eating, drinking, conversing and speaking tongues glorifying God! The twenty-four elders are also at the Wedding feast along with Mary the Mother of Jesus. In the Sanctuary the Almighty gets ready to perform the ceremony! The Angels gather up to make the Heavenly Choir to sing doing the Wedding. The Sanctuary is decorated with fabulous colors to represent the Lamb of God Lord Jesus Christ. Jesus the Bridegroom is dressed in all white. He is flanked by two Arc-Angels who are serving as Best Man. Music that normally plays to worship the Almighty is paused and Wedding Music began to play. Gabriel blows his Trumpet and the Saints rise up in one accord and rush into the Sanctuary all dressed in fabulous white ready to march down the aisles. The Sanctuary is filled with many Angels all gazing with so much love! The Heavenly Choir began to sings *What God has join together let not man put asunder!* The Saints which is the Church walks down the aisle quickening in the power of the Holy Ghost. They are speaking in Tongues! Glory! The Almighty Fabulous face shines so bright no mortal person can stand in His presence. Jesus stands on the right side of His Father watching as the bride which is the Church marches down the aisle. Once the Bride reaches the Altar a beautiful creation of the Almighty (which took the place of Lucifer) began to sing a wonderful solo *Bonded Together for Ever!* After the Solo the Almighty begin the ceremony! Jesus vows to take the Church to love & cherish forever!

The bride agrees with a powerful glory! Speaking in Tongues glorifying God and the Lamb. All the Angels in the Sanctuary began to worship the Almighty! God shall say to His Son, "*Give them the ring of ownership.*" Jesus gives the Church (which is a number no man can number) a fabulous diamond ring signifying ownership. Jesus says, "*With this ring I wed thee!*" The Church says, "*Hallelujah!*" Then Almighty declares, "*I pronounce you man and wife*. The Father speaks to His Son, "*You may kiss the bride.*" Jesus obedient to His Father kisses the Saints and you talking about a falling out by the power of the Holy Ghost! WOOWEE! Saints slain by the power speaking in tongues! Saints get up so drunk in the Holy Ghost! He grabs hold to an Angel and the Angel began speaking in Tongues by the power of God! The Wedding music ceases and music resumes to worship the Almighty. The Saints drunk in the Holy Ghost start dancing by the power. All the Angels starts dancing! WOOWEE! Some shouting going on! Praising God! Jesus is dancing with the Saints! Glory! Glory! Glory! God's beautiful creation plays some music in worship toward God, while the Heavenly Host are dancing!

Some people may wonder why the Sanctified people dance and shout so much in Church? This is the reason because dancing like that goes on in Heaven! God is a God of the living and NOT of the dead! Jesus bring joy unspeakable and full of glory! The Saints continue dancing shouting and praising God. The Angels also are shouting and praising God! The Holy Ghost even grab hold of the twenty-four elders and they were drunk in the Holy Ghost! Mary the mother of Jesus speaking in tongues glorifying God! The beautiful creation in charge of the music department is also speaking in Tongues glorifying God! Praises goes toward God who sits on His Throne.

The Church gather together after the praise with Crown of life on their head. The ring on their finger signifies married to the Lamb of God sweet Jesus! Forever together with my love! God speaks saying, "*Now you can go on the Earth to live for a thousand years.*" Jesus takes the Church and prepare for their journey to the Earth.

B. Millennium

After the Earth is cleansed and the wicked is cast into Hell. Satan and all the demons are chained and cast into the bottomless pit. The key is brought up to God who is in Heaven by the Arc-Angels. Jesus shall bring the church to live on the refurbished Earth. It shall be beautiful just like the Garden of Eden in the Bible. The Earth will be full of life with all types of Creatures in land and sea. It will be a very peaceful atmosphere with no thought of evil. Lions, tiger, crocodiles, bears, sharks, eagles will not be predators but all will be vegetarians. All the Saints which is a number where no man can number shall live with Jesus for a thousand years in perfect peace. They will be able to travel from one end of the Earth to the other. Swim in the deepest oceans without any fear or getting tired. Children shall play all in the rivers and streams without any fear of drowning. The reason there is no such thing as death! Death is swallowed up in victory! Glory!

Jesus shall reign on King David's Throne in Jerusalem which is in Israel. All the Saints shall communicate and love each other all over the Earth! During the day God's lovely face can be seen smiling on His children. The Saints feels so safe! There is no such thing as feeling bad or thinking a negative thought! Just peace, happiness and joy. I mean to tell you it will be impossible! I say impossible for you to think of anything negative! The reason you are married to sweet Jesus. Satan and all the demons are locked away in the bottomless pit so all the evil is gone!

Children run all around on the Earth having a great time. Jesus appears all around the Earth visiting his people. The Saints are always happy to see sweet Jesus! The Saints enjoy all the beautiful flowers, plants and trees. They love all the creatures. They live-in houses just like former Earth. These are beautiful mansions with lovely plantations. There is no such thing as poverty for all the Saints are rich in the wealth of the Earth. Everyone enjoying each other rejoicing off everyone progress! Saints shall work together to get the Earth going again.

Inventions such as flying cars, high rise houses will be built. Fabulous bridges, skyscrapers for major cities. God shall give them knowledge to light the houses, bridges and cities at night. During the night it shall be a spectacular show of lights to decorate the night! Angels shall desire to look at the work of the Saints of God. The sky will be filled with the Angelic Choir singing songs of unto the Almighty! The Saints on Earth will worship the Lord God doing the night and day! The Sun shall shine doing the day and the moon will shine at night along with the stars. God's smiling face shall be seen doing the day within the Sun.

During the night the Saints shall rest and there shall be tremendous peace in the valley with no such thing as restless nights, depression or nightmares. Jesus shall make His rounds all around the Earth visiting the church both night and day. All of His visits will be seven times better than Christmas Day! How do you feel celebrating Christmas all year long? That is how it would be when sweet Jesus be visiting with the Church. When Jesus is in the midst something good is going to happen!

The Nights upon the Earth will be spectacular with heavenly light shows of Stars shinning so bright! These shows will be seven times greater than a fireworks display here on Earth. Even the Almighty who shows His fabulous face in the Day will talk softly at night to make the Saints feel at peace and safe! On the Earth will be a very large Temple in Jerusalem where all the Saints can come and worship the Lamb of God Jesus and His Father the Almighty God who is up in Heaven. There will be plenty room for the number that no man can number. Saints who are all over the world will come to this one Temple in Jerusalem for worship! Songs will be sung to the Lamb of God so glad they have been washed in the blood of Jesus. Saved from sin not to sin anymore! Shouting and praising God for eternal life! The Saints all dressed in white with the fabulous crowns of Life upon their heads.

The Temple will be filled with dancing, shouting and praising God! Music will be played by the leading of the Holy Ghost and the Saints will be quickening by the power of God. Jesus shall sit on His Throne in the Temple. Angels shall play the music just like up in Heaven. Jesus shall smile when the Saints testify how He delivered them from the traps of Satan. So much joy will be going on! Services will be going on in the Temple each day. Traveling there will be so easy far faster than you can blink your eye you will be around the world! That seems impossible with the knowledge of man. Please understand this, God's technology is far beyond man's knowledge.

The Saints will love to be in the presence of who their soul loves which is Jesus. Attending the Temple will be much joy and excitement! Each time at the Temple is tremendous joy! Jesus will speak words of life to energize the Saints of God. They will all go up in a praise which will reach Heaven! Father God will receive the praise as a fresh fragrance! The Almighty God will breathe in the fresh fragrance and bless all His Children. He will speak in a soft lovely voice saying, "This is the work of my beloved Son in whom I am well pleased at all of my children." This will cause the Holy Ghost to fall heavy from Heaven to rain just like a heavy downpour all over the Earth. All of God's creatures along with the Saints will be drunk by the power of the Holy Ghost. The Temple will be full of speaking in Tongues; praising God in various languages! The Creatures on Earth will be praising God in their own way from the ants on the ground all the way to the Eagle that flies in the air. There will be no such thing as violence of any kind!

The Saints shall exit the Temple faster than you can blink your eye and go to their different sections of the Earth! The whole Earth will go up in a worship unto God up in Heaven. This highly pleases God! The Saints shall enjoy peace for a Thousand years!

After the thousand years the Almighty God shall speak to the Arc-Angels to take the key and unlock the bottomless pit! The Arc-Angels go down and unlock the lid of the bottomless pit and the chains came off of the old Dragon Satan. He comes out of the pit and sees the Saints enjoying perfect peace on Earth. He sees Jesus on the Throne of His Father King David. He is cursing and speaking blasphemous words because the Saints are married to Jesus and he can never speak to them again or put any negative thought in their minds! All of this beautiful world Satan wants to destroy it with evil! So, he vows his revenge! Satan goes out and gather up all the demons which were locked up with him and gets ready to make his attack! Jesus alerts the Saints and all get their swords along with the Angels and Arc Angels of Heaven. TIME FOR WAR!

C. Battle of Armageddon

Satan and all the demons shall rage one final battle with the Heavenly Host and the Saints of God. War will be intense with all the Earth destroyed! It will be a war the world has never seen. Jesus will empower His bride to fight with tremendous strength! They will put heavy blows against those very demons which tormented them while on former Earth! They will be fighting hard against demons who had them in slavery, depression, fear, poverty and those demons who false accused them. They will fight against cursing and lying demons. Demons of alcohol, drugs and witchcraft. Even demons of illicit sex, homosexuality and lesbianism. Those Saints who were beheaded on Earth for Jesus' namesake will be fighting those demons.

The Arc-Angels will be fighting hard against Satan! This fighting will show no mercy, but fight to destroy! Anger shall be intense against Satan and all his demonic forces! Angels shall also be in battle fighting those demons along with the Saints! During these battles the Saints and Heavenly host will not get injured or hurt in any way for they are shield by the power of the Holy Ghost! Satan and all his demons will suffer tremendous blows from the Saints and the Heavenly hosts! The Saint will enjoy as they knock those demons up side the head! One Saint kick them on the side! Punch them so hard the demon lost their balance and fell down!

Jesus teach His bride how to box and give
those demons a knock out punch!

The Holy Ghost will empower the Saints to give
those demons a final knock out punch!

O demon of lust a knock out punch! Demons of laziness, greediness and lust of the flesh will be fought by the Saints. A demon who encourages the Saints to dress like Jezebel in earrings, lipsticks, gold chains, tight clothing to show their shape the saints will beat him down really good. The demon who encourages divorce will be attacked by the Saints. Other Saints will be fighting demons of the love of money! There are thousands, thousands of demons! So much fighting will be going on!

The beautiful Earth will be destroyed along with plants and the animal's breath of life goes back to God who gave it! This battle will be one for the ages! All the Saints will rejoice giving God the praise as they beat up on those demons! The fighting will go on until Satan and all his demons are beaten down! Then the Arc-Angels put them all in guarded condition and take them up to God for Judgement. This brings me to the Resurrection!

D. Resurrection

There are two Resurrections the First Resurrection and the Second Resurrection. The First Resurrection takes place at the Rapture of the Church from the Earth before the Marriage of the Lamb of God and the Millenium. That is when Jesus takes the church out of this world and present them before God up in Heaven as a chaste virgin. The Saints will be given brand new glorified bodies which will never die or sin! These new bodies will come from these old earthly bodies. The Saints will get ready for the Marriage of the Lamb. The Second Resurrection is for the wicked and those who died in their sins refusing Jesus as their Savior.

The Almighty shall order the Angels to gather up all the dead. The Earth and Hell shall give up all the dead to come and stand before the Almighty to be Judged along with Satan and the demons. They will see the image of the Almighty but His face will not be seen! They will see Jesus sitting on the right of His Father. They even see the Saints of God all sitting dressed in all white behind Jesus! Each name will be called by the Angel who has the Book of Remembrance. The Almighty shall say, "*Review their life!*" Their whole life will be put on open display for all to see! It will be far better than any movie made in Hollywood, California! These scenes shall be just like you are actually living in that time! The only difference is everything is exposed. Even the thoughts of man are exposed! Nothing is left out! No matter how embarrassing it is it does not matter! If you did it, will show!

When God sees all the evil His anger grows HOT! The Spirit, the blood and Water does not agree for their Salvation through Jesus. He asked is their name written in the Book of Life which is controlled by the Angel. The Angel checking the book says, "NO!" Then the Almighty shall say in a roaring voice stronger than seventy E-F Tornados "On the left side!" The Angel shall move them to an area which has a large net. There will be many scenes of evil such as adultery affairs, fornications, witchcrafts, smoking, drinking alcohol, stealing, defrauding, prostitution, dancing at clubs, idol worship, masonic worship, false religions, love of money, jealousy, deceit, hatred, using illicit drugs. Those who commit murder, robbery, burglars' scenes will be shown.

Slavery was all judged by God by those who enslaved their own race in Africa. Black people enslaving Blacks, their abuse of beatings, sexual harassments, rapes and murders. Those who molested children and beat them keeping them from eating food drinking water and medical care. The evils of Slavery were judged by God in the United States of the Caucasians on the Black people. Their beatings, sexual abuse, rapes and murders. The evil treatments of the American Indian were also judged. All the Indians wars, race riots, lynching and evil executions were all judged by God.

All family incest were also judged by God. Relatives saying, "*This is our little secret!*" On this the Almighty's anger kindle hot! Every *secret sin* is judged by God, nothing is left out! Those who done evil and escape punishment from the law of man because they had money, powerful position etc. were judged by God. The one who commit murder of individuals and turn the weapon on themselves taking their own lives. Now the world feel they got away with it, because the dead don't know nothing! That is what they say. That is NOT what God says. Their evil deeds are judged by an Almighty God. What is done in the dark are brought to the light!

The assassinations of *Julius Ceasar*, United States Presidents: *Abraham Lincoln, James Garfield, William Mckinely, John F Kennedy* and even *Robert Kennedy* and *Martin Luther King* Jr. will all be viewed by God. The evils of the Jewish Holocaust will be viewed by God. All the evils done by *Adolf Hitler, Joseph Stalin* and other world leaders are exposed in the open seen by Almighty God to be judged. Every unrepented evil act will be exposed and judged by God. Nothing, I say again Nothing will get by! The very secret things in which man kept hid in this world are exposed before an Almighty God! Every person mistreated, who is guilty of it and did not repent while in this world are brought up before God.

Members of racial hate groups such as *Ku, Klux, Klan* and the *Black Muslims* are brought before God to be judged. The Almighty shall say in a roaring voice, "*I am a God of love for all races of people. I created all nations by one blood. I have no respecter of person.*" When they heard that they will be speechless! Those who are guilty of robbing, abusing the poor will be brought before God to be judged. False Clergies who loved money more than God will be judged by God. They refuse to preach the whole truth of the Word of God but preached watered down doctrines so they can draw the crowd and money.

The Antichrist along with the False Prophet and beast will be judged by the Almighty! All of their evil activities will be examined by God. God will see how they lived their life on Earth leaving out God Almighty but ran the world on man's ideas. The Anger of God grew hot with the Antichrist for teaching the people to worship the Science of man, teach evolution that man came from Apes. The Antichrist taught people the law of man was to be feared and God up in Heaven is invisible. We cannot see Him, so He does not exist! The news media, schools, universities and medical science all teaches Man is god of himself. They worship the Antichrist who is the man of sin. When the Antichrist saw the image of the Almighty and heard His Powerful voice, great fear gripped his heart! Even all the atheist in the crowd was dumbfounded at the glory of God! They only could see His image but could NOT see His face! The Antichrist looked and saw Jesus sitting on His Father's right hand along with the Saints of God sitting behind Jesus. The Antichrist spoke saying, "*Jesus I heard the Romans killed you!*" Jesus answered saying, "*The Romans did not kill me! I voluntarily laid my life down and I picked it back up again!*" When the Antichrist heard this, he was speechless! The false prophet cried out, "*This must be a terrible nightmare! There is no life after death! The dead know nothing.*"

The Almighty spoke in a roaring voice, "*Thou fool! I am a God of eternal life! In me there is no such thing as death!*" The False Prophet was speechless. Jesus said unto the false prophet, "*My Father's anger is hot against you for misleading the people away from God down the path of destruction.*" The False Prophet was accused for seducing the people to that lady Jezebel to worship her by painting their faces and decorating themselves in gold, earrings, rings and nose jewels. This which leads to witchcraft which is wicked in the eyes of God!

The Almighty God heard enough and ordered them to go to the left side. Their names are not written in the Book of life! The Arc-Angels push them on the left side with the great crowd.

After Judgement has finished the Almighty shall say unto all those on the left side, "*Depart from me all of you who work iniquity. You are cursed forever in everlasting Fire prepared for the devil and his angels.*" People in the crowd began to scream in fear! Others began to accuse and say, "*Your laws are too hard for us to do! We are free to choose!*" Then others began begging, "*Lord please give us another chance!*" Jesus shall say unto the crowd,

My Father's commandments are not hard if you love Him. The way you lived your life refusing my love and mercy continuing to follow Satan proves you have no love for God in your heart. I gave you a whole lifetime to repent of your sins and you refuse to repent! You refuse to listen to my servants, but mocked them! Why should I give you another chance?

The Crowd shall say, "*What about my good deeds. Don't that count?*" Jesus shall say unto the crowd, "When I was sick you visited me not, thirsty you gave me no drink, hungry and you fed me not, stranger you took me not in, prisoner and you came not unto me, naked and you clothe me not." The crowd shall say, "When did we see you thirsty, hungry, naked, sick, homeless and in prison?" Jesus shall say, "*When you refuse to serve my little ones you refuse to serve me!*" Jesus pointed to all of them who dressed in white sitting in the stands behind the Throne.

The Almighty shall say, "I have seen enough!" He waves His powerful hand and all of those on the left side received bodies which can stand intense heat! They were trap for eternity! The Almighty commands the Arc-Angels to take the Crowd away to outer darkness. He raised His mighty hands and cause blindness strike the eyes of all in the crowd. Truly they were all in outer darkness. By the wicked gazing at the image of God cause blindness to come to their eyes! The Arc-Angels picks the blind crowd up in a net like bag and travel throughout space into outer darkness. There are millions, millions of them! They arrive to a distant star. The Star opens its mouth and the Arc-Angels throws the large Crowd into the Hot Fire! The Star grabs all of the Crowd swallowing them into the Hot Fire!

Screaming like never before will come from the crowd as they enter into those Hot Flames! Nothing but Fire! Fire! It is impossible for them to escape! In the Fire they cannot see because of blindness! Naked souls rolling in Fire continue falling but never hit the bottom! The Star swallowed the Crowd down into the base of the Star. There they will remain for eternity! They will NEVER burn up! Always burning in Hot flames! Their bodies will have them trapped and it will stand all that intense heat! In other words, it will NEVER break down! They are locked in throughout eternity in Fire! Fire! Fire! It will NEVER go out!

After the Arc-Angels dump all the crowd into the Star, it closes its mouth engulfing them on the inside. The Arc-Angels return back to the Almighty for the Judgement of our old enemy Satan and all the fallen angels. Satan is finally brought up along with the fallen angels. The Almighty anger is extremely hot! The Almighty spoke in a roaring voice, "Satan you have cause much havoc destroying my work and stealing my creations of man to turn against me! For all of this you MUST pay!" Satan was shaking in tremendous fear! All of the fallen demons were also shaking with tremendous fear. I say there were thousands and thousands of demons. The Almighty gave command for His Son Jesus and Arc-Angels to take a whip laced with thorns as sharp as nails and beat Satan and all the demons. The Saints of God watched as Jesus and the Arc-Angels began whipping Satan and all the fallen angels. The beaten was very intense. Satan and all the demons cried out in so much pain! The flogging continues and the Almighty laughed along with the Saints of God as Satan and the demons were flogged! They flogged them until they were all crushed down.

Then the Almighty command saying, "*Satan your vision shall leave you to never return along with all the fallen angels.*" The Almighty waved

His mighty hands and blindness came upon Satan and all the fallen angels. Satan is permanently blind and defeated! God commanded for the Arc-Angels to take Satan and the fallen angels and cast them all into the lake of fire! The Arc-Angels take up Satan who is blind and weak. They also take all the fallen angels also blind and weak and carry them to their eternal punishment. The Almighty shall say, "*The angel of death I have no need of you so take him and cast him into the lake of Fire also.*" The Arc Angel takes death and carry it along with Satan and the fallen angels.

They travel back to that star in outer darkness. The star opens its mouth and the Arc-Angels cast Satan and the fallen angels into the Fire. They all went in screaming the star swallowed them right up to be forever lost in the fire! Then the Arc-Angels took death and threw that into the fire. When they threw death into the fire. It gave the fire power to torment the lost souls with sickness, sorrow wishing to die but cannot. This will go on for eternity. After death is cast into the lake of Fire, the star closes its mouth. The Arc-Angels seals it with a special seal from God. This star is to be seal for eternity! Jesus shall allow His bride to observe all the activities from a distance! These Saints shall recognize their own cousins, uncles, aunts, parents, husband, wife, co-workers, friends etc. who did not receive Jesus as their Savior. They will be all crying out in pain burning in the intense heat of the flame. Jesus will not allow you to cry, but instead you will rejoice and give God the praise you are so glad you made your escape.

After the Arc-Angels complete their task, they are return back the Almighty and tremendous joy will be in Heaven. The Almighty will say, "I will have a world where all my creation will know is to do right nothing negative will come in their minds! There will be nothing around to make them feel bad, depressed or cause them to frown. I am a God of love, peace and joy!" All of Heaven shall worship the Almighty and give glory to the Spotless Lamb of God the Lord Jesus Christ.

CHAPTER 13

Spending A Vacation In Heaven

The very heart desire of every true child of God is to spend an eternal vacation up in Heaven to live with sweet Jesus, God Almighty and all the Heavenly host. This is a dream that will one day come true unto all believers in Christ full of the Holy Ghost and Fire. Every believer who has this hope will purify themselves in this life and be pure as Jesus is pure. Once you make it into Heaven walking throughout the different levels you observe all the beautiful green meadows and rich green grass. There are the beautiful waterfalls, so full of life flowing gracefully down the mountains into the rivers. There are many beautiful flowers in so many colors. The smell of the flowers is sweet. Saints are enjoying smelling the different flowers without any fear of allergies like on planet Earth. You look and observe strong healthy Trees so tall up in the air! A Saint can climb the tree and see all over Heaven!

Mountains and hills are very beautiful. As you climb the Mountains you can see the beautiful valleys below. The scenery is endless, beauty beyond this world. The Flowers sway in the wind singing praises unto the Almighty! The wind blows whistling praises unto God! The power of the Holy Ghost acts as a cool breeze. The streams and rivers are crystal clear. They are so clear you can see the bottom. Rivers, streams have strong current and are full of all God's beautiful creatures. Fish of all kinds, Whales, octopus, crocodiles and allegators. (These creatures are different than the ones on Earth. For the Lord God made them all gentle as a lamb). No wild nature whatsoever.

You may ask the question do animals go to Heaven? Yes and No. Yes, the breath of life of all living creatures both man and animals return back to God who gave it. Unlike the animals on Earth man has a soul. That is what makes man above the animals. The breath of life returns back to God who gave it and God give the life to another one of His creatures. You must know up in Heaven there are no natural bodies all are spiritual supernatural bodies for the creatures. All the Saints are spirits in Heaven waiting for God to give them their supernatural spiritual bodies in the world to come. There is only one person who has His supernatural spiritual body that is sweet Jesus who is our High Priest next to the Mighty Throne of God.

As you look up in the sky there are many flying creatures. White Horses with beautiful white wings flying through the air! Birds of all kinds with beautiful colors! An Angelic Choir appears singing praises to the Almighty. All the Birds, flying horses sing praises unto God. God's smiling face can be seen shining brighter than the Sun warming Heaven with so much love and kindness!

Just like I stated earlier in my book Heaven is divided in three levels on Earth Clergy and the church only tell the congregation portions of the truth about Heaven. Some say if you make you just going to make it! That is True but I am going to go further:

A. First Level

On level one you observe the beautiful Apartment Buildings. These buildings are made with granite marble stone. All the Saints lived in so much peace. These Apartments are so beautiful with furniture that are elegant and stay brand new all the time. Saints are satisfied glorifying God and the Lamb of God as they decorate these Apartments. The Saints on level one is dressed in glorious robes of worship and praise unto God. The robes are comfortable and never gets dirty. They wear a beautiful Crown of life along with golden shoes which are so beautiful they shine brighter than light!

Jesus makes his appearances on this level and the Angels flies around bringing joy, peace and love! The atmosphere above is filled with

Glory and praises unto God. Saints on this level are busy doing their assigned task. There are many tasks to get done such construction of new Apartment buildings. These buildings are tall like the buildings in *New York City USA*. After the buildings are erected, it is decorated on the inside. The walls are decorated with fabulous designs glorifying the Lord God. There colors are like a rainbow! The walls are made of marble stone and floors are polished sparkling bright and clean!

The stairs are also made of marble stone. How do you like walking up the stairs shouting, *"Glory to the Lamb of God!"* As you move up in the building you can hear people inside the Apartments praising God in their own way! Singing will be going on and wonderful inspirational conversation. Someone will open the door and say, *"God bless you, my child! Would you like to come in and visit?"* These Apartments are furnished with fabulous furniture which will last for eternity. Luxury chairs that Kings and Queens would use in their palaces on Earth. Tables are made of very best wood. It is all polished and sparkling! Windows are made of marble stone with glass. Cabinets are made of fabulous wood which will last throughout eternity. Walking in these buildings will put you in mind of walking in *Buckingham Palace* in *London, England.*

As you reach the top of the building there is a recreational area where the Saints can relax in chairs, get together and sing a hymn to the Lord God and unto Jesus the Lamb of God. The Angels who enjoy looking at all this marvelous work will come down and visit the Saints in these Apartment buildings. The Saints will relax in the chairs on top of these buildings and they will bless the Lord as they look up and see God's smiling face!

These Saints are thankful unto Jesus for saving them from eternal punishment in Hell. Apartment buildings are constantly being built for all those who JUST make it into Heaven! It is a chance I would not take because Satan is NOT playing. He is fighting hard to keep every soul OUT of Heaven. These cases of individuals who are near the door of eternity and Hell Fire is their destiny one more opportunity is given unto them to repent and they accepted Jesus as their Savior forsaking the world of sin. Jesus wonderful forgive them of their sins, sanctify them to the blood and baptize them and fill them with the Holy Ghost and Fire.

They reach Heaven Jesus presents them unto God a chaste virgin to receive their crown of life. They are dressed in glorious robes of worship and praise unto God. The Angels gives them golden shoes. They are so glad, they made it into Heaven. Their place of assignment is the first level. It is the First level a soul can say one moment in God's Kingdom will pay for all the suffering down here on Earth.

Every new arrival that comes into Heaven enters the First level. The Angel meets them and escorts them straight through the first and Second levels all the way to the Third level to the Tabernacle not made with hands to meet with the Almighty God.

When Gabriel blows His Trumpet, all from the first level go to the Tabernacle not made with hands. They are assigned in a special section near Jesus. Jesus pours love on these individuals and the power of God slays them out by the power! They are drunk in the Holy Ghost causing all the Heavenly host to go up in a dance before the Almighty! Music is played glorifying God. The Almighty smiles and the Holy Ghost fall like a heavy rain!

There are wonderful green pastures loaded with herds of *sheep, cows, bears, lions, birds, monkeys* and other creatures. Mountains high and valleys are so beautiful. Crystal clear rivers, streams and ponds full of marine life! Beautiful flowers full of sweet fragrances. The animals are friendly. *Dogs* and *cats* are wonderful pets. Birds will fly to the windows of the Apartments and the Saints will enjoy their singing praising God! The dogs and cats run in and out of the apartments. The Saints enjoys them so much!

It is a great honor to live on the first level! They will have great joy and strong desire to serve faithfully the Saints of God. It gives them tremendous joy to serve the Saints on the Third level. The Saints on the Third level honor them blessing them with wonderful gifts of love! Saints on the Second level and the Saints on the third level will visit with the saints on the First level glorifying God!

B. Second Level

This level is beautiful with Mountains, rivers, streams and hiking trails. Saints can enjoy themselves looking at all of God's wonderful creations. Angels sails through the air singing praises unto God causing all of Heaven to sing. Flowers of many different colors and fragrances sway in the wind of the Holy Ghost singing praises unto God. Tall trees are so high a Saint can climb and see all over the different levels of Heaven.

The Saints on this level are dressed in glorious robes of love and mercy. While on Earth they stressed much during their Christian life on Earth that God is love and is a forgiving God. They are all given golden shoes that shine brighter than light. They wear their Crowns of life. On this level God has given them glorious Townhouses unlike the Townhouses on Earth. These Townhouses are built with precious stones and filled with elegant furniture. Walking in these Townhouses is equivalent to walking in the *White House* in *Washington DC USA*. Throughout the Townhouses you can hear conversations of praises unto God! When you visit the Saints there is much joy and positive conversation. All visits are wonderful and the Saints are eager for more.

The walls of the Townhouses are painted with many colors like a rainbow. The Saints decorate their Townhouses with much joy and excitement! The Saints are very happy they made it into Heaven! They give praises unto God and the Lamb of God. Jesus makes His appearances all through the Second level. There is not any sign of jealousy or feeling bad! These Saints fellowship together on one accord with much love and glorify God!

There are many streets loaded with Townhouses made of very best brick material. The walls are made of marble stone. Floors are polished sparkling bright. The stairs in the Townhouses are made of the very best wood overlayed with soft material for carpet. This is a very good carpet which will last throughout eternity. The Saints will take charge caring for the carpet. The atmosphere is full of life as the birds come to the windows and sing songs glorifying the Almighty! Creatures in the fields bow to the Almighty who smiling face shows in the sky! It is so wonderful as the Saints from all levels flies through the sky under the watchful eyes of the Almighty! Some of the Saints goes hiking through the Mountains and down in the valleys. Others go running along the trails viewing the wonderful scenes of the animals and beautiful flowers with so many colors.

These Saints on the Second level will have their special section in the Tabernacle not made with hands. They will be next to Jesus the Lamb of God. The power of God shall work in them causing them to be quicken in the Spirit. They will help Mary the mother of Jesus to lead the Church in praise and worship. God will task all of those on the Second level to work as subjects under the leadership of those on the Third level.

The Second Level of Heaven housed all those Saints while on Earth gave their heart to Jesus and doing their Christian walk with the Lord gave into Satan temptations of Flesh causing God not to be totally pleased with them. They rather to spend money going on trips to the beach than to sacrifice money to feed the poor while on Earth. "*Let the government take care of them! I have to spend my money on my family.*" This attitude displeased the Lord God! They love to be in the media attention while on Earth drawing praises of men! The people would pack their churches and hear watered down messages telling them to repent of their sins. Preaching unto them the Baptism of the Holy Ghost but refuse to warn them to forsake the forms and fashions of the world. They loved money more than warning them to forsake the world.

In all of this God is not totally pleased. Thank God, they made it into Heaven and have a place in God's lovely Kingdom. God is highly please now there is no sin in them! His smiling face shines on them in the Second level. All new arrivals travel with the Angel through the Second level of Heaven.

C. Third Level

This is the goal that a true Child of God want to live. It is here where God's beautiful Throne Room and the Tabernacle not made with hands. The Beautiful City with tall Solid Gold buildings. Gold plated streets made of glass where you can see yourself as you walk on it. Mansions built with Diamonds, Emeralds and Pearls! All the Mansions overlaid with solid Gold! All of these Mansions are gigantic with many rooms for the Saints to decorate!

The third level is prepared for those while on Earth dedicated their entire life unto God. They lived a life free from sin through much mockery, ridiculed and abuse from Satan through people! They suffered much persecution on Earth and some even died a martyred death for Jesus. There were those who suffered much poverty and died on Earth of starvation or disease. They are all comforted up in the Third Heaven!

Saints shall live in rooms made of pure gold. The stairs and windows are also made with gold. The glass in the windows is crystal clear the Birds fly there to sing praises unto God. There is so much *gold, sapphire, silver, emeralds, diamonds* and *pearls* in this level. The Streets shine like transparent glass! It is exciting to be walking up pure gold stairs inside of gold buildings! There is so much gold that it is fascinating! You walk into one of the rooms and see all those gold walls floors all polished and shining like glass! Chairs, tables, cabinets all made with diamonds, emeralds and pearls. I understand some people reading this may say, "*This sounds too good to be true!*" Know that God is Almighty and He has ALL the riches of this world in the palm of His mighty hands.

The Saints are friendly and full of conversation. They are ALWAYS glad to see you! The Lord gave me a vision of me standing in the Third level of Heaven talking to some people I knew in the church. *Brother Henry Spence, Brother Willard Barkley* and *Brother Samuel Thomas*. They were looking so young and *Brother Henry Spence* could see so well! That is a great blessing because the time I knew him on Earth he was handicapped with blindness. We were all in the spirit just as alive more than the people here on Earth!

On the roof top the Saints can sit in their chairs and relax blessing the Lord God who is up above smiling shinning seven times brighter than the Sun! Pleasant conversations going on talking about many things that are encouraging! Laughter! Happiness! Peace! Gabriel blows his trumpet and the Saints rush into the tabernacle not made with hands to worship the Lord God!

In the Tabernacle the Saints from the Third level fill the Sanctuary in front of the Almighty! The Children gather in the children's section. The first and second level Saints are next to Mary the mother of Jesus which is beside the Lamb of God. The Almighty looks at the Third level Saints with great love because they expressed their love for Him while on Earth! Heaven honors the Third level Saints! Stars just like you see in the Universe will be placed in their crowns of life! Those Saints who brought souls to Christ and they reached Heaven a Star is placed in their crown. Many Third level Saints are walking around heaven with more Stars than others! It is exciting to walk into someone who tells you. "*Listen you may not know me while we were on Earth, but when you where preaching on Radio. I heard your message. You said a prayer at the close of your broadcast. One day you said that prayer I ask Jesus in my heart. That is why I am here in Heaven today.*" Another person will say, "*You didn't know while on Earth I saw you preaching the Gospel on television. You would preach your message and say a prayer at the end. One day you said that prayer I ask Jesus in my heart!*" You will run into many people who will tell you how you touch their lives through your ministry.

The Lord God will give Stars to those on the Second level who faithfully shared the Gospel and souls believed and came to Jesus. These souls reached Heaven. God is highly pleased. Those on the first level gets no Stars! All is so glad they made it into Heaven! That is reward enough! Yes to escape a burning Hell is reward enough to celebrate for eternity!

Just like I stated earlier in my book, God is going to reward those who dedicated their entire life to Him from their youth and serve Him faithfully until they lived a very old age unto death. They lived a life NEVER tasted alcohol, tobacco, drugs and not guilty of fornication or Adultery.

Saints while on Earth suffered poverty, forsake the fashions of this world. Some even gave up watching Television, going to the beach lying nearly naked, gave up going to the amusement parks, watching ball games and fellowshipping with the world at family reunions and parties. They were mocked and abused called insane! Some suffered their marriage destroyed because of their faith in the Holiness of God. Their spouse left them went out and committed adultery. They stayed faithful unto God even unto death.

These Saints are ridiculed of all people on Earth. Satan try to make life miserable for them by causing people to look over them for promotions on the job in the military or whatever they do. Even when these Saints die at their funerals nobody really shows up! There are only a few people. The world counts them as nobody!

God has highly exalted them in the Third Heaven! He has given them a wonderful Mansion so beautiful and shines brighter than the

Sun! Each Mansion has the Saint's name on it! Those Saints who have not arrived in Heaven but are still on Earth has a mansion building but is not yet finish! The Saints who are already in Heaven sees who Mansion is being built and when one is ready. Once a mansion is ready those Saints who know that individual while on Earth runs to the First level entrance Gate to greet that individual because that is signal, they are coming home!

Saints from the first, second and third levels all come together and help decorate the homes on all three levels! Great fellowship and everyone are so happy! There is NO SIGN of any jealousy, hatred or anything to make you feel bad. Just peace, love and joy! This is a wonderful, wonderful time! Jesus makes His appearance and God smiling face shines so bright over the Third Heaven! All the Saints up in Heaven are Save and Jesus holds them fast and it is impossible for them to get away! I want to ask the Question who wants to get away from a loving Savior as my Sweet Jesus? The Angels up in Heaven gaze over all this activity with much love!

D. The New Jerusalem

In the Third Heaven is the **New Jerusalem** that great City of God made of beautiful buildings of Gold with Gold shinning streets. This wonderful City will be descending down out of Heaven to the New Earth which will be coming for the Saints of God. **Revelation 21st Chapter** the Tabernacle of God will come down and dwell among His people.

Heaven is a very busy place full of activity. Downtown Heaven is just like any city on Earth, but without the traffic accidents, motor vehicles, traffic lights or airplanes. Everybody is control by the Holy Ghost! They are so Courteous and giving each other the right a way! Arc-Angels walk along the streets with the Angels and Saints! There is NO thought of evil! Glory! Glory! Glory! Everything is so new, clean and not a speck of dust! Once a soul reach Heaven you will see THIS is the real world! This Earth where you came is only temporary! Along the streets there are many, many shops with beautiful merchandise, flowers, pictures and beautiful materials. Each shop is operated by an Angel! You may ask what do they use for money? The Saints goes in and shop picking up all they need.

When they go to the counter to add of up their costs, the Angels smiles and says the price has already been paid! Jesus paid it all for you! Jesus suddenly appears and joy began to flood your soul!

Saints from all levels come downtown to shop and pick up materials they need. You may ask how do they transport the materials? There are cherubims all throughout Heaven with many flying horses with chariots and they do all the transporting of materials throughout all the levels of Heaven. There are also shops with recreation materials for the children. The shops are loaded with balls, many games and other recreation materials for children to use to play. The Angels are all in the shops with smiling faces serving the saints. The atmosphere is so lovely! Saints are talking with other Saints. Saints are talking with Angels. Angels are talking with other Angels.

Just like I said, there are no traffic lights in Heaven. So, at the very busy intersections in downtown Heaven. God place a very beautiful Angel which directs traffic. At all these intersections the Saints are all full of patience and glorify God as the other Saints passes by! The Schools are downtown Heaven. All the Schools are built very large! They are larger than any University here on Earth. Angels works as teachers and professors. Both children and Saints are taught many things that are never taught here on Earth. In these Schools no student makes any errors! They absorb all knowledge like a sponge! They passed all tests, exams with a perfect score of 100 percent. There is no such thing as failures! Every student excels in these Schools!

So much activity goes on in Heaven. Angels gather up Students to take them on a field trip going way out into outer space to see God's wonderful creations. They study distant stars, planets, asteroids. Some study the weather of God in all the precipitation of rain, snow, hail, thunderstorms, hurricanes, tornados. wind, low and high pressures. There are so much to do and so much to see up in Heaven! In all the activity Gabriel will blow his trumpet! When the trumpet sounds that is signal for all of Heaven to report back to the Throne of God! Everybody rushes into the Throne room in a moment of time! Worship and Praise began as we bow unto the Almighty! God's Throne are brilliant with great colors, beautiful rainbows. The Music in the background give His Throne excellence and power! The Saints does not fear God because there is no sin or no such thing as an evil thought! God smiles with love! The Lamb of God sits on His right hand! Mary the mother of Jesus sits on a seat at His right hand. Mary magnifies the Almighty God and Jesus Christ her Savior. All of Heaven acknowledge Mary as the Mother of Jesus. (They do not worship Mary) Mary leads the church in worship unto the Almighty! God's powerful name is spoken and all of Heaven shakes in honor! Angels and the Saints quickening in the Holy Ghost giving God the praise as His magnificent name is spoken! All the creatures throughout Heaven bow in reverence to His powerful name!

The noise is great that it reaches the depths of Hell and Satan is knocked off his Throne of Rock and forced to bow! It lightens and thunders down in Hell each time God's name is spoken up in Heaven! All the demons and devils tremble with tremendous fear, for it is a reminder of that dreadful day which will come to cast them out into outer darkness in the lake of everlasting Fire forever!

The Saints rejoice and gives God the praise and worship the Lamb of God Jesus Christ! Dancing and shouting go on more than you can imagine! Joy! Joy! Joy! Everlasting joy! Can you imagine being excited with joy all the time? Can you imagine feeling great without a care to worry about all the time? All of this is possible up in Heaven! This is the real world! Everybody is so happy all the time! If it is possible that anything about to come and take away that joy Jesus immediately intervenes and takes it away! Up in Heaven it is NOT possible! Jesus makes sure all the Saints are always happy! Singing, testifying and praising God goes on! Everyone enjoying each other! Saints are hugging, smiling and showing great love. Jesus even hugs the Saints and those hugs makes you feel good on the inside!

After the Lord God showed me all of these things I have written, I truly do understand the reason those Sanctified Holy Ghost Filled Pastors preached strict Holiness during their lifetime on Earth. I take time to get honor to those strong Holy Ghost Filled preachers in my life: *Eldress Lillie P Williams, Bishop Rufus A. Easter, Bishop William Easter, Bishop Randolph Artis, Bishop Elisha Whitley, RW Schambach, Apostle Johnnie Washington, Eldress Rosa Banks* and *Mother Elnora Jarrell.* They stood strong that you live free from sin in this sinful world. They preach give sin all the way up and give up the world. Obeying preaching like that will get you a reward of entering into the Third Level of Heaven.

Satan will encourage Christians to obey those Clergies who teaches Christians to compromise and take down during things that the old saints would not do. Famous saying, "*It's not no harm.*" It may not be no harm now but when you face eternity, it could become an issue on what level you will be on in Heaven. Some Christians will say, "*I don't believe in levels.*" They want something for nothing! They feel they can enjoy the world confess Christ, repent when they commit sin and inherit the Third level of Heaven. Do you really think God going to allow you to treat Him like that? Time to wake up Christians!

E. Types of Angels

There are different types of Angels in Heaven: One type are the **Arc-Angels** which are the highest Angels empowered by the Almighty to fight against any opposing force! These Arc-Angels have the power of a hundred nuclear bombs explosions. Man, and all his technology is no match to one of these Arc-Angels. Satan and all the fallen Angels are no match to one of these Arc-Angels. The Arc-Angels does the fighting against the opposing forces of darkness. They surround the Throne of God and guard the Tabernacle not made with hands. The Arc-Angels make sure Heaven remains perfect place just as God made it! Each Arc-Angel is dressed with amour and given a powerful sword! They patrol all around Heaven!

Arc-Angels are power creations by God equipped ready to fight the powers of darkness. They are constantly at War with Satan and the fallen Angels.

143

The next type of Angels in Heaven is what I called the **regular Angel** which is dressed in white with beautiful wings. They are the ones which work in different shops, prayer room, serve as messengers at the Throne of God and does many other tasks the Almighty needs done. These Angels are empowered seven times stronger than the fantasy character Superman on Earth. They travel from Heaven to Earth and return to Heaven. They constantly get in a battle with Satan and all the demons. They can fight and the battle can go on for days, weeks, months or sometimes years by Earth time. God looks down and see the Angels having trouble, dispatch an Arc-Angel to come and give the Angel a hand fighting the demons.

An Angel of the Lord who serves as Messenger of
God. Photo by tatlin from FreeImages

The next type of Angels are the **little Angels with childlike faces** these Angels minister constantly at the Throne of God singing songs of praises unto Him. They sing all over Heaven hymns and many songs unto God! A child like Angel can be sitting along the hike trail and begin singing a Spiritual Hymn unto God. Once the little child sing all of Heaven will join in and sing a song. This means all levels, in the shops, schools no matter where the Saints are they will join in and sing unto the Lord God a song of love and worship! Jesus the Lamb of God will attend the schools and call all the children to come unto Him. Once they come, He blesses them and the power of the Holy Ghost cause them to speak in tongues! These young Angels are dressed in white and have beautiful White wings. They remain in Heaven until they grow into **regular Angels**.

The children, Angels, Arc Angels are innocent and know NO sin! All they know is the righteousness, holiness of God! God takes all the souls of babies which die at birth or after birth on Earth once they get to Heaven let them grow up in Heaven with one of the Saints who had no children while on Earth. God will give some babies to Saints who are gifted with loving to have children.

Some babies are made into childlike-face Angels to minister unto God in the Mighty Throne Room. The Babies up in Heaven do no crying like of those on Earth. There is no wrong or danger to be afraid. Heaven is the safest place for any person to be!

Child-face Angels are in Heaven serving The Almighty God along with the Lamb of God. Photo by Jacob Cole from FreeImages

CHAPTER 14

The New Heaven and Earth

A. The New Earth

When people say God is good! I MUST say YES! YES! YES! God is good! In Heaven God is constantly talking to the twenty-four Elders sitting around the Throne. Together fabulous plans are being made for all His children. God wants to create worlds where all His children can live. He wants to take His children and make Rulers over nations of people. All these worlds will be populated with creatures of all kinds just like former Earth. Plants, trees, flowers of all kinds will be abundant! They all will live throughout eternity! The Rulers God will pick will be those who suffered for Him faithfully while on Earth! Those who were persecuted and died a martyred death for the name of Jesus. God will pick those who faithfully served Him from their youth up to a very old age! Even those who loved Him so much to win many souls for Him while on Earth.

He will place beautiful crowns on their heads making them Kings! This crown will be in addition to the crown of life! All Saints who won souls to Christ during their life on Earth a Star is added to their Crown of life. Some Saints will have more Stars than others. Those who are Rulers in the newly formed worlds will have their Crown of life changed to include the Crown of King. All Saints will know that Saint is chosen by God to rule over that group of people. The Saints assigned to that nation will love their leader and all will worship the Lord God in the Heaven and sing praises unto the Lamb of God.

In these new worlds Saints shall be free to travel without the means of Technology on former Earth. They can fly like the fantasy character *Superman*.

The Saints can travel flying around the New Earth
like the Fantasy Character Superman

They can run fast like the fantasy cartoon character *Flash*. The Saints will be able to visit and travel all over the world. They will fly over large bodies of water in minutes. Everyone will be happy to see each other! The Lord God will cause the New Earth to bring forth Vegetables, Fruit and Nuts of all kinds. It will serve as food. All of planet Earth will be like the Garden of Eden! The Lord God will help the Saints create large cities and have fabulous Mansions made of precious stones, Gold and Diamonds. Everyone will be wealthy and poverty will not exist!

The Saints' eyesight and hearing will be phenomenal. They can see perfect for miles and miles. Their hearing shall pick up the softest of sounds. Their health will be excellent both physically and mentally. All will live forever!

The Almighty shall say, "*I want all my children to be prosperous in gold, diamonds, emeralds and pearls. Let their riches be without measure. Let their crops grow healthy, green to nourish their new supernatural bodies.*" God shall bless all His creations to live on throughout eternity. This Earth will be much larger than former Earth. There will be plenty of space for the great number of Saints where no man can number!

The Great City of God the **New Jerusalem** will be descending out of Heaven down on the New Earth along with the Tabernacle of God. The Holy Ghost will live among His people. God loves perfection and He desire a Universe, Earth that never touched sin! That is why it is NOT good for Christians today to play with sin. The only reason we can get into Heaven is because of Jesus who gave His life on Calvary, so we can come OUT of sin! God loves a person who is FREE from sin! ONLY the pure in Hearts shall see God. **St. Matthew 5:8** Jesus shall reign on Earth as the KING of KINGS. All the Rulers God make over the nations on the Earth shall come under the KING of KINGS which is Jesus! The whole Earth population including all of God's creations shall lift their voices and worship the Lamb of God Jesus Christ King of Kings and Lord of Lords! Saints shall cast their crowns to the ground, bow and worship Him.

The Rulers who were made Kings shall cast their crowns on the ground and worship the KING of KINGS! Jesus! Jesus shall sit on the Throne of David in the New Jerusalem City in the new world. Everyone in this world will only know Righteousness. Not ONE evil thought will come to their mind! All in this world is righteousness! There NO such thing as sickness or accidents. There will be no such thing as *I trip on a table and hurt my leg! I fell off the tree and broke a bone. The Lawn Mower cut my finger!* Everything will be perfect! Each Nation the Saints who are made Kings shall rule with much love. All the other Saints shall work under them with love. There will be no such thing as anyone taking advantage of someone! No such thing as someone abusing anyone! No such thing as gossip, backbiting or thinking evil of anyone! All evil and negativity will be history and forever forgotten! This whole world will be filled with righteousness!

All the creatures will be full of love. All shall live forever! Children shall play in the beautiful forest without any fear. They will jump off tall buildings and float to the ground. Just like I stated, there will be no negative thought such as pushing someone off a tall building or a cliff. Children will play innocent! All the Saints will work together in perfect harmony! The Lord God will give them knowledge to grow all types of vegetation for food. There will be nuts and other types of food that was not on former Earth. God will give His children knowledge to make great inventions such as to help make life easy in this new world. The inventions they will create will last on into eternity. There will be nothing in this new world which will wear, rust or play out. This will be different from inventions of man here in this present world. How would you like an oven range, dish washer to work forever and not ever play out? In the New Earth that is God's amazing plans for His children.

Great Buildings will be built of gold, silver, other precious metals and stones. The cities are full of beauty! Out in the country shall be full of life with beautiful fields of crops of wonderful vegetables and fruit. In this new world there be no hot deserts, no cold north or south poles. The weather all over the world will be warm not too hot or too cold. Perfect weather all the time! Skies are beautiful with no threat of violent weather such as Hurricanes, tornados, thunderstorms with hail or heavy rains like the monsoons on former Earth.

This new world will have no blizzards or any freezing weather. The Lord God will cause a mist to come up out of the Earth to water the Earth. He shall give His children knowledge to get water out of the rivers, streams for the people to drink. There will be no need to purify it like former Earth, because all the water will be one hundred percent pure. God will have all His children to return back to the Earth what they taken out. It will continue in a cycle. There will be no misuse or abuse of what God has created. All creatures will be treated with love. There will be no abuse of any creature. Even the fly or spider will not be harmed, for they will respect all of God's children and will not hurt them in any way!

Ticks and all bacteria will be friendly to man. There will be no such thing as germs! All bacteria in the microscopic world will be kind. Birds of all kinds will fly through the skies the Lord God will have them return to the Earth in a proper place. They will not lay no bird droppings on none of the Saints, children or any of their possessions. The Birds will take care of their business in a proper place! All of God's creatures will live forever. No bird, spider, ant, tick or bacteria will die. Death will NOT even exist!

Jesus shall be present all over the Earth securing all of His children. God the Father who is up in Heaven shall smile with great pleasure when He looks and sees all of His creation living in perfect peace in Holiness and Righteousness. It is wonderful for the Saints to go about their daily activities enjoying each other with much love. It is wonderful being on the job, enjoying Jesus singing songs unto the Lord God. The more you sing the better the activities go. People decorating in the buildings working together talking positive conversations. Angels from Heaven flies through the sky looking down at all the activities on Earth with much love!

The Lord God shall have the New Earth just like former Earth rotate on its axis causing day and night. The Saints shall be busy doing the day and rest at night. During the night Angels from Heaven will fill the skies singing praises unto God. The Almighty God shall show His magnificent face! It shall cause a great praise to come out of the Earth! Glory to God in the Highest! Peace on Earth! Love unto everyone. When Gabriel sounds his trumpet everyone on Earth regardless to what they are doing resting at night, working doing the day, in the mountains, walking in the parks, shopping in the malls, riding the subways, in the schools etc. shall come to a stop and rush to the Tabernacle over in Jerusalem to meet with Jesus! The Tabernacle will have a big worship service praising the Lamb of God Jesus and sending praises up to Father God in Heaven! Glory! It will be so much shouting, dancing, speaking in Tongues the Angels of Heaven will love to watch! Their praises reach Heaven it will be a sweet-smelling savor unto the Almighty! After service Jesus shall let them go and in a moment of flash exit out back into the different parts of the Earth going back to their activities.

Everyone in this new world will be worry free! Feeling good all the time! There will be no thought of taking any drugs or smoking any plants to get high! All the Saints will know to do is right in the eyes of God.

Saints shall turn on the radio in their homes, vehicles and the only music will be inspirational, Holy Ghost music and praises unto God! No bad news will even exist! Always good news. Someone will get on the radio and speak some marvelous words from Jesus which will go all over the world. That is the difference in radio waves in the new world unlike former Earth where the waves have limits with the exception of shortwave and satellite signals. These radio waves will have strong signals similar to short wave signals or satellite signals on former Earth.. No matter what the waves are: amplitude modulation, frequency modulation it will cover the entire world. Any time of day or night, the saints will be able to turn on the radio to hear an inspirational message from the Lord. Jesus shall even speak on the radio unto His bride from Jerusalem. Glory! Glory! Glory! Beautiful singing praising the Lord! Hallelujah!

How would you like for six days out of the week having conversations, doing activities with those who love the Lord! Every time you see them, they are so glad to see you! You will NEVER hear, *"Don't bother me! You are worrying me! Or Get out of my face!"* It will be impossible for them to even frown at any of their fellow Brethren. Jesus will give you joy unspeakable and full of glory! All the Saints who were assigned to all the different levels of Heaven will be assigned to their positions on the Earth. Those on the first level will be assigned as messengers delivering items to the Saints all over the Earth. Some will serve as servants for the Lamb of God! Glory! They will be dressed in a glorious white Robe with a wonderful crown of life on their heads. Those on the Second level of Heaven are assigned to help prepare feast for the Saints of God and Lamb of God. They are also dressed in glorious white robes with a beautiful crown of life on their heads. There will be great nations upon the Earth. Kings, Presidents and Emperors will be assigned by Jesus unto those who went to the Third level of Heaven. These leaders shall live in fabulous mansions built with solid gold! The Saints shall all have great love for all their brethren. All Saints shall always be welcome to their mansion. Visiting will be so wonderful. So much positive talk for there will be NO negative talk or thought! Laughter and so much joy will be going on! All saints along with the leader will be looking so young at the age of thirty-three years old. They will remain young throughout eternity. Only the children will grow in the new world until they reach thirty-three years old, then they will level off.

Jesus shall constantly make His appearance all throughout the Earth seeing after His children. The Angels will constantly come down and visit with the saints. The Lord God shall give saints on the second and first level knowledge to create fabulous inventions. They will create machines to process vegetables and fruit. They will create machines to fly and even drive on land. Saints will drive all around the Earth in automobiles and there will be NO accidents! Accidents will not even exist! Airplanes shall fly without any such thing as an accident. Airplanes fly high up in the sky just like former Earth, but unlike former Earth if the saints jump out of the plane, they will float down to the ground without a parachute! You will land so gently! There will be no fear of gravity! Only fear the Saints will have is to honor and respect the Lord God up in Heaven.

The Lord God shall give the saints knowledge to create big companies to provide different services for the Saints. These companies will work together as team. **Greed will not even exist!** One company will specialize in making pancakes mix and another company will specialize in making the syrup! Each Company will look out for the other Company. There will be NO one company buying up all the contracts leaving others with none. All large companies will allow small companies to operate and make a profit. They will rejoice at each other's success! The spirit of emulation will not exist. All will be helpers of one another. The companies shall be manufacturing clothes, automobile parts, airplane parts, cereals. There will be no manufactures of medicines or any drugs! All the factories will be manufactures of produce, furniture and other services the Saints needs to live. The smoke coming from the factory will not be toxic like it was on former Earth. It will be clean, pure smoke! Glory!

The fuel for the factories, cars, ariplanes and other motor vehicles will be pure, clean fuel to help the environment. Air, water or any type of pollution will NOT exist! Air is crystal clear! Fire will not be like the Fire on former Earth. It will only warm, cook and do all the positive things to help mankind. It will NEVER get out of control and burn things like former Earth. It will NEVER burn or take someone's life. The people of

God and even the Children will NOT be afraid of this fire. Just speak to the fire and it will obey you! Say, "Fire burn here." The Fire will burn. Say, "Fire don't touch that part of the house and go out in an hour." The Fire will do exactly what you say! Glory!

There will be interstates, freeways and other highways busy with commercial traffic trucks carrying products to different stores in cities and towns to supply the Saints. It will be pleasant traveling on the interstate and all on the road will be traveling for Jesus. You need not to worry about traffic speeding, reckless driving or accidents will not exist! All will be done to the glory of God. This is true trucking for Jesus!

Tractor trailer hauling products and services all in the mighty name of Jesus. Free Images photo

There will be no hospitals, clinics, doctors or psychologist. The health of everyone will be excellent. There will be so such thing as having a bad day! No such thing as high blood pressure, diabetes, blindness, deafness, broken bones, sprain ankles, cancer, common colds, influenza or COVID-19 virus. There will be no police, fire department or rescue squad. No jails, prisons, lawyers, judges or courts. Funeral homes will not even exist! No need for guns, laser guns, nuclear weapons or any bomb because there will be no death, killing or destroying anything! No military because there will be no WAR! Just Eternal life in a world full of activity. Cities large as *New York city, Chicago, Ill, Tokyo, Japan* and *London, England.* with subways, buses and many people walking the streets. All fuel stations will be on welcome greetings for the Saints to come and get fuel for their vehicles. All currency will be gold and silver. There will no price hikes or greed. No such thing as a fuel shortage. All will be in abundance! All business shall be one hundred percent honest. Shoplifting will not even exist for all stores will be surrounded by the power of the Holy Ghost. Cities and towns will have mayors appointed by God from the Saints on the Third and Second levels. There will be many, many shopping malls busy with Christian businesses and many people. Everyone is walking, talking speaking to each other saying, *"Praise the Lord!"* God shall give the Saints knowledge to be excellent bakers to make fabulous cakes and pies! They shall bake apple, peach, cherry, peacan, coconut custard and many other flavors. The cakes will be mouth watering such as: Lemon, Chocolate, Strawberry, Banana and Pound cakes to name a few. The saints will eat these wonderful desserts with many types of frostings. There will be all types of puddings, jellos and whip crème. All desserts will be finger licking good! They all will remain fresh! There is no such thing as spoilage!

The Lord God shall give them fresh milk from the cow and goat. They have no need to pasteurize or sterilize it because the milk will be healthy and clean for human consumption directly from the cow and goat. The Lord God will give them food which will taste like all the meat they ate on former Earth. Food which will taste like hamburger patties, Fried Chicken, Bake fish, T-Bone Steak, Leg of Lamb etc. This food will be healthy life everlasting food far better than all the meat dishes you can think about on former Earth. It will be finger licking good! It will cause people to live thousands, thousands, thousands of years and keep on counting! Someone will say, *"Lord bless I am 12 Thousand years old, look just like I am thirty-three and feel so young!"* Glory! People will be celebrating birthdays in the thousands, millions, billions of years and so on! Glory!

Ice cream will taste so good with its favorite colors of Vanilla, Strawberry, Chocolate, Butter Peacan etc. Streets, malls and business will be crowded with people! All activity goes on until Gabriel blows His trumpet. That is when activity ceases, business closes and everyone rush to the Big Temple to worship the Lord God and His Son Jesus Christ. Many languages are spoken fluently and all Saints will know how to speak many languages with so much ease. Many songs are sung in several languages filling the whole Earth with the joy of the Lord!

Just imagine a world with no such thing as crime! Businesses, offices, factories, homes will not even have to lock your doors! In fact, the doors are left wide open and nothing negative happens! In this world there will no such thing as adultery or fornication. All Saints will do what is well pleasing unto God. Profanity or evil thought will be unheard of. Truth and honesty will be the only thing which comes out of the mouths of the Saints of God! Imagine walking down the street to greet someone saying, *"Praise the Lord! How are you doing?"* The saint responds, *"Glory! I am doing great thanks to the sweet Jesus!"* It is normal to look and see a Saint shouting, speaking in Tongues walking down the street. In this new world there will be no such thing as someone trying to take advantage or abusing someone kindness. All Saints will love each other just like they love themselves. They will have respect one for another!

The Lord God shall allow His children to build fabulous mansions with several floors. These mansions shall be built with pure gold, and other fine metals. Rooms filled with good furniture. Floors polished with great wax shinning so bright! Saints shall have mansions seven times more beautiful than the King's Palaces such as Buckingham Palace in the United Kingdom &The President's White House in the United States of America on former Earth. Every child of God will be the owner of several mansions. Throughout eternity the saints will be constantly having new Mansions being built! All mansions will be filled with people. Saints will enjoy moving from city to city, town to country, planet to planet. The real estate will be full of buyers all over many planets the Lord God shall create. All purchases will be one hundred percent honest with the best deals. Everyone from all levels will enjoy the wealth God shall give all his children. How would you like to own mansions built in solid gold on several planets? How would you like to own fields full of fabulous crops of butter beans, corn, sweet watermelons, canteloupes, oranges, apples, strawberries, peaches and so many other good fruit and vegetables? All of the people will enjoy going to the fields picking pears from the pear tree, corn from the stalks, fresh butter beans, collard greens, spinach, blackeye peas, garden peas, watermelons from the gardens. Oranges from the many, beautiful orange trees. The trees are so loaded with oranges that they will fall to the ground. The children will enjoy picking up the sweet tasting oranges to take with them to school. There is no such thing as a sour fruit! Even lemons will be sweet instead of sour like former Earth.

Fresh bananas, peaches, apples that will never rotten! Plenty food for everyone! These are the surplus which did not go to the market. God give his children so much in abundance! Plenty for all! Saints who goes to the market will have plenty of produce to buy at great prices! God will give all those who run businesses a great profit! They will be satisfied and shout, *"Hallelujah!"* The evil spirit of greed does NOT exist! Everyone will enjoy everyone's wealth of mansions and land. Everyone will love to share what they have will others! Angels will love to come down and see all of God's wonderful work done here on the planet. It will be normal to see Angels visiting the fabulous mansions of the Saints. Jesus shall makes his appearances at all the mansions on a daily basis. Joy will fill the air! Love is so abundant!

The Lord God shall give man knowledge to create power to operate machines, appliances and light for homes, businesses in cities, towns and in the country throughout all planets. Many large cities will look so beautiful than any Christmas Tree on former Earth. The one Temple of worship on the planets will be lit up shinning so bright at night. Jesus will be King of Kings ruling on all planets. The Saints will be enjoying life traveling from planet to planet. Living in their Mansions of Gold, Diamonds, Emeralds and Pearls. Kings, Governors, Mayors and all officials on all planets will bow and worship the Lamb of God who is Jesus the Son of God! Their praise will reach Heaven unto God the Father, who is well pleased! The Holy Ghost will be super strong on all planets.

The Holy Ghost will guide you all the time! Glory! Just as I already stated, in this world Saints can drive on land and in the air accident free! There is no need for seatbelts for all Saints practice safety at all times! There is no need for traffic lights, stop signs or speed limit signs. All Saints will stop at all intersections look both ways before proceeding. They will travel at proper speeds all the time. The reason is all are control by the power of the Holy Ghost! Glory! Although God shall allow the Saints to install in the New World Traffic signals at intersections. These signals along with walk signals will be obeyed with upmost care! In this new world there will be no such thing as red light running or jaywalking.

Plenty of traffic all going in the mighty name of Jesus! Free images photo

Everyone will be so polite looking out for one another. Driving down the road yell out of the window, "*Praise the Lord Saint!*" It is Honk if you love Jesus! Many Honking of car horns going on in Jesus' name! A

Saint riding the motorcycle every time he gets a chance shout *"Glory to the Lamb of God!"*

Go walking and you see the *pottery shop*. Inside there are workers who make beautiful flower vases, plates, cups, bowls and other things of clay! There will be no such thing as breaking a cup, vase, bowl for all vessels if drop on the floor or ground it will be like falling on a soft blanket! There are many schools, universities where children learn many things in Science, Math, and other subjects. Education will be far above all the education on former Earth. There will be very intelligent children and adults. Their IQ intelligence will be seven times that of *Albert Einstein*! They will be able to explain very tough questions and solve incredible hard math equations! God shall give them wisdom seven times more than King Solomon on former Earth!

All nations shall be united in tremendous love for each other! They shall love their leader who is king or President. The Lord God shall allow the Saints to vote for their leaders He has already approve. There will be no cheating of elections like they do on former Earth. All elections will be honest! When one candidate wins all rejoices! In fact, there will be a great dance unto God in the streets! Everyone congratulating the candidate who won! So much happiness! A great feast will be given for all to attend! It will be a Hallelujah time! Saints are fellowshipping with one another and giving praise unto God!

Each time a new leader of a nation is chosen the whole Earth goes up in a praise unto God! All nations shall have a democratic government all in Righteousness. All Saints from the Second and first levels will be treated with high respect! They will be given gifts for all their faithful work. These gifts can be silver, gold and pearls. In this world everyone is Somebody! Nobody is left out!

All things done will make everyone happy! There will be much laughter and working trying to make their nation beautiful! Children running all around the streets in cities, fields in the countries. Children are playing down in the rivers and streams! Fields are full of healthy crops of corn, string beans, butter beans, pinto beans and other vegetables. There shall be many fields full of beautiful strawberries, cherries, and other berries. Watermelons and cantaloupes shall be so plentiful. Nuts such as *Walnuts, Brazil, Peacans*, and *Hickory* all healthy and good for the

Saints to eat. Peaches and nice juicy apples are on the Trees. There are many beautiful flowers and soil so rich and fertile.

All the mansions on Earth will be cool at the right temperature all day and night throughout the year! The week will be seven days. Every Sunday is automatic Church Day and the whole world closes down for Sunday Church services. Anytime during the week if Gabriel blows his trumpet all the saints will come together to worship the Lamb of God Jesus! Church services are wonderful full of shouting, dancing and praising God! Jesus will be blessing the Saints in the Tabernacle on Earth. All their praises go up to Heaven before God who is very pleased! The Lord God will be so pleased that a cloud will encircle the Temple and the voice will speak out saying, "This is my beloved Son and all my children in whom I am well pleased!"

All shall be comfortable with the weather seven times that of the State of Hawaii on former Earth. There shall be Holy Ghost anointed baseball, soccer, kickball, football games. The Saints will play friendly loving games. They will be many homeruns hits, touchdowns, and goal wins doing these games! No matter what team scores, all will go up in a praise to the Lord God up in Heaven saying, *"Glory unto God almighty and to Jesus Christ!"* The moment they speak Jesus. He appears right there in the field blessing them! The players will be speaking in Tongues in the Holy Ghost! Glory! How would you like a ballgame when a player hit the ball it is a home run? Every time a player on the Football field run the ball, it goes to a touchdown!. God shall give everyone different abilities and they all will be perfect in His sight. All players will join together and help each other reach the goal. This will be for all baseball, basketball, volleyball, hockey, and soccer games. How would you like a see a baseball or softball game where all the bases are loaded?

The team put up their player who hits a home run and all the players come running in home making scores! The crowd goes up in a praise toward God; all the players on both teams goes up in a great praise and celebration! Dancing on the field praising God! Everyone is enjoying themselves and having a great time! There are no Mascots or idols displayed but all honor and worship the Lord God Almighty up in Heaven and Jesus the Lamb of God. Angels shall look over them at the football, basketball and baseball fields. All is done to the glory of God.

These ballgames will be joyous and the Saints will be glorifying God! Every player will enjoy themselves so much because they will get plenty of exercise! After each ballgame a big celebration goes on with so much joy! Jesus will appear at the celebration blessing the players. These are ballgames in the new world where both teams are winners! In this world there are no losers! Glory! The Angels of the Lord shall walk among the Saints in the New Earth for in this world there is no sin! Glory! Everything is so good. Even the waste material the Saints and animals put back into the Earth shall not smell foul like on former Earth. It will be pleasant and easily blend back into the Earth because nothing shall be wasted.

B. The New Heaven

The New Heaven the Lord God will create bright Sun to shine on the Earth during the day. He will create moons and stars to shine on the Earth at night. The Lord God shall let the Saints take trips into space to visit all of His creations. There shall be many glorious colors to beautify the Universe. In the third Heaven the Almighty shall have a Tabernacle not made with hands replaced all built in pure gold. The Sanctuary is gigantic all polished shinning bright ready for the Saints to assemble. The Almighty Throne is still something wonderful to gaze full with many bright colors. God's glory lights up all levels of Heaven! The city in the Third Heaven is replaced with another city just as beautiful. All the schools which were up in Heaven are now on Earth. Mansions of the Saints on the first, second and third levels are now in the Earth. Heaven is beautified with wonderful flowers, trees and other plants. Many fields rich in green vegetation. The Almighty shall look and see all His work and His only begotten Son Jesus sitting on King David's Throne on Earth and shall be well pleased. In all His work, He sees no sin! God magnificent face shall be seen on Earth and all the Saints shall bow in honor to the Almighty along with animals and everything that has breath.

The Saints along with the Angels shall leave the Earth and go up and visit the Almighty in Heaven. Traveling from Heaven to Earth shall be the life to live! No matter where the Saints are Jesus will know where to locate you! You can be on a distant planet in space, in the bottom of the ocean on Earth, up in Heaven with the Almighty. Jesus will always know your location! Angels shall look down from Heaven to the Earth singing praises unto God. His name shall be spoken and all Heaven and Earth shall bow to the Almighty! Jesus shall honor His Father up in Heaven. All shall sing songs in honor of the Lord God. Then shall the Saints no matter where they are shall sing songs to the Lamb of God Jesus Christ. NO SIN OR NEGATIVE THOUGHT SHALL EVER CONTAMINATE THIS WONDERFUL ATMOSPHERE!

I know this is hard for some people to believe, but this is true! There will be no argument or misunderstanding on anything! No greed, gossip or backbiting! Everyone speaks truth and always something positive! There will be no such thing as thinking evil about anyone! All people will be smiling showing their wonderful white teeth! Smile O happy smile. All conversations on the telephone will be holy conversations speaking in tongues to their brothers and Christian businesses. All the saints shall drink wonderful, clear cool water! Plenty of it! Peace so much peace! Nothing in this world to make you even think of something negative or to make you feel bad in any way! Glory! Glory! Glory! Saints will enjoy righteousness all throughout eternity! They shall walk boldly in the presence of the Almighty God in Heaven! The Almighty will enjoy them so much for what will come out of their mouth will be righteousness and wonderful things glorifying God!

C. The Cold Planet

The Lord God in Heaven will allow all His children to travel deep through space to a planet which will show His magnificent power of beautiful snow! This planet will have freezing temperatures and the snow will be marvelous! The Saints will be shield so the freezing weather will not affect them. In fact, there will be no such thing as freezing to death! The Lord God will allow the Saints to build Igloos which will keep them warm. The Saint will build campfires and sing songs unto the Lord God and to Jesus Christ the wonderful Lamb of God. This planet will also be busy full of all sorts creatures: *mouse, deer, bears, foxes, rabbits, hawks, eagles* and they will eat the fruit and nuts buried in the snow. On this planet there will be towns and cities as big as Chicago, Illinois on former Earth. There are shopping malls busy with people. They will drive on the road through the ice and snow will NOT have an accident! They will be riding in their snowmobiles.

Saints will be driving snowmobiles around glorifying God!
Photo by <u>Shalom Pennington</u> from <u>FreeImages</u>

There will be no slipping up on the ice! It will be far better than Christmas time on former planet Earth. Everyone will be joyous singing songs worship the Lord God!

The snow will fall beautifully. It will be quiet and full of peace! Love all over the planet! Jesus will make His appearance all over the planet! The Lord God up in Heaven will show His face through the clouds at night smiling at His children. Snow will be on this planet all year long and Saints will come and go! Children will be ice skating on ice covered ponds without any fear of ice breaking! All will be giving sweet Jesus the praise. Some of the Saints will be so amazed for they never seen snow before. The Lord God will empower the Saints to be able to ski on the snow-covered mountains! There will be many long ski trails! The Saints will be skiing to the glory of God! It will be normal to hear someone shout "*Glory!*" as they ski down the trails! Although the snow is beautiful, it will be so enjoyable watch the children to play in the snow. They will even shout, *"Glory! To the Lamb of God!"*

The Saints will enjoy skiing down the snow-covered trails
glorifying God! Shouting Hallelujah to the King of Kings
Photo by <u>sheldon pickering</u> from <u>FreeImages</u>

There will be no such thing as snow ball fights, building idols such as snowmen and other images! Although beautiful Igloos will be built! These Igloos will house Christian business and other services. The Lord God will empower the Saints to dig into the ground to bring out precious resources of metals, oil and other materials to build fabulous houses. There shall be day and night on this planet. The Sun will shine during the day and the moon at night. Saints will be arriving and departing the planet. Jesus shall be there all the time! The Saints feel so much at home. Not a worry or negative thought around. Fear do not exist! Just peace, happiness and joy!

All these worlds the Saints life will be busy and full of life! The Angels singing praises in the skies at night among the clouds of snow! Saints on the planet will all speak in unison saying, *"Glory! Glory unto God Almighty!"* Saints will be busy until Gabriel blows His Trumpet. Once that Trumpet sounds. All Saints wherever they are will quickly exit and be flying to the Temple on the new Earth to worship the Lamb of God and God Almighty. I must say the hearing of all the saints is phenomenal in that they can be on the cold planet and still hear Gabriel blows his trumpet. Their eyesight will be phenomenal in that they can see people clearly many miles away! The Saint will not have anything to worry about because what they need is being taken care of.

In these worlds there will be no need for a fire department for there will be no such thing as a fire getting out of control. There will be no liquor stores, no tobacco stores, no smoking or getting high on any plant or substance! There will be no gambling or magic shows of any kind. All that is done will be to the glory of God. Just imagine riding a subway full of people speaking in tongues praising God! Walking in the airport and people are praising God, listening to Gospel music, or talking to sweet Jesus. It will be normal to be riding in a plane and a saint will be flying through the air like superman! How about sailing on the ocean and children are playing in the bottom of the sea? I am telling you these worlds are so friendly and it is nothing like former Earth!

As the song goes *If Everybody Had Jesus What a Wonderful World it Would Be* will come true! Another song Streets of Innocence will be true among all the children! There will be no such thing as a spoil child! Children will be gentle, loving and obeying the Lord in all things! You will never hear anyone correcting a child for all they do will be right in the eyes of God! There will be no crying in Heaven nor the new Worlds for all will be full of joy! Everyone is having a great time traveling all over the world or going to the cold planet and even some goes up to Heaven to visit with the Almighty! You may ask *"What will happen if Gabriel blows his trumpet and the Saints be flying in the airplane? Will the airplane crash?"* Good question let me explain in this perfect world it is impossible for an airplane to crash so when Gabriel blows his trumpet for the Saints to come to the Temple. The plane will immediately land on the ground and the Saints will vacate the plane to meet Jesus. Even if the plane is flying over the ocean, it will immediately get to land so the Saints can go to church! Glory! Those Saints who are in Space will quickly leave to come to church!

There will be so much dancing, shouting and praising God in the Temple. Mary the mother of Jesus will be leading the church in praise and worship! The Angels sings in the Choir and plays music with many musical instruments. Guitars, trumpets, tubas, drums, organs, keyboards, cymbals, cowbells, scrub boards giving God the praise! All these praises reach Heaven and come before the Throne of God with the twenty-four elders. The Almighty is so please and commands His Son to bring the church up here. Jesus and the church leave the Temple on Earth and go up to the Sanctuary in Heaven to have worship service with the Almighty. It is exciting to go to the Tabernacle not made with hands. In this Tabernacle there is no prayer room for the Saints need not to pray for Jesus now is with them always. The Holy Ghost will have His way in their souls and bodies. It is amazing to gaze into the Glory of God with many beautiful colors! So much beautiful singing with the Saints and Angels! Jesus the Lamb of God joins with His Father in Heaven. Mary the mother of Jesus sings, "*O how my soul do magnify the Lord God! My Savior Jesus Christ!*" The whole church falls in with her magnifying the Lord God and Jesus Christ the Lamb of God.

In the Tabernacle the Almighty shall share with all of Heaven some of His magnificent plans. It will be exciting news. All the Church will be listening with interest. All the leaders of Nations will be there taking in all of what the Almighty is saying. The Lord God shall create a wonder in Heaven to amaze all. A wonderful creature to magnify the Lord! It cries, "HOLY! HOLY! HOLY! HOLY! All of Heaven bows down and worship the Almighty crying, "HOLY! HOLY! HOLY! LORD GOD ALMIGHY! THE EVERLASTING GOD!" The Lord God has so many good things to share with His Children. He will be laughing and cause the Saints to laugh! The Almighty shall create many solar systems of Earths for man to live on. All shall be righteous and Holy before God. When the Saints heard this, they worship the Lord God saying, "*Whatever you do is good my Lord! Glory to the Lord God Almighty!*" The Saints shall call the Almighty by His Holy name and it will cause the power of God to shake Heaven mightily! A great dance of praise will come causing the Saints and the Angels to shout before the Lord. Even the great Wonder Creature joins the Saint shouting and praising God! Glory!

The Children shall be recognized by the Almighty for their accomplishments such as Graduations from Schools, Colleges and Universities. It will be a great honor for God to recognize the Children! When the children march before the Almighty. they will be dancing by the

Holy Ghost causing the Church to dance. The Almighty shall pass out the Graduation awards. These awards will be fiery stars placed in their crowns. When the children received the awards, they will be speaking in tongues magnifying the Lord! The Saints shall all clap their hands in joy! The Angels shall rejoice along with the twenty-four elders. Dancing and shouting praising God going on in Heaven. Great music will be played glorifying the Lord God whose name all of Heaven speaks which cause a great shaking!

God shall assign the children tasks to do in the new world. They will be scientist, those who build bridges, invent vehicles to ride on land, sail on sea and fly in the air. They will be great builders who will put up great buildings in the new world. God shall also send some Children to build beautiful igloos and fabulous buildings at the cold planet.

Fabulous igloos will be built by the Saints on the cold
planet Ice Hotel Photo by marmit from FreeImages

The Lord God shall share with all His children His wonderful plans of having worlds of life. All these plans fascinate the congregation. Then the Lord God shall say unto His Son Jesus. *"Take your bride back to the New World and continue with the wonderful work you are doing."* Jesus and the church exit Heaven and return back to the Temple on Earth! The Shouting and praising God continues and Jesus rains the power of the Holy Ghost among the mass congregation! Angels sing songs in worship unto God up in Heaven. Much music is played by every instrument you can imagine and those instruments you don't even know about. Music belongs to God! Fabulous music is played even when the service dismisses from the Temple and the Saints return back to their different tasks on the Earth. The beautiful inspirational music goes on through the air on the radio.

The Cold planet will be so full of activity. People walking on snow covered streets in their winter clothes. Snow coming down so beautiful and as you walk look up into the Heaven and bless the Lord God! The streets are loaded with so many of the Saints always greeting and having wonderful smiles. As you walk into one of the shops you observe fabulous grandfather clocks, appliances for the kitchen, radios, (there is no need for television because The Angels, Jesus and God Almighty put on such a wonderful display at night it takes the place of such inventions). Ranges, Refrigerators, freezers, dishwashers and trash compactors are all in these shops. There are fabulous stores equivalent to *Sears & Roebuck, Montgomery Wards, JC Pennys, Macys, Walmart, Targets, Lowes* and *Home Depot on former Earth.* How would you like to walk in a department store equivalent to Burlington Department store and shout, "*Glory!*" The Clerk shout "*Praise the Lord!*" The cashier goes off in a dance before God? Yes, all of this and more besides will be going on in the Cold planet and the New Earth. You walk into a store equivalent to Sears and the salesperson greet you with "Praise the Lord!" Shopping will be joyous being among the true Saints of God! You will be getting all honest sales on ALL quality merchandise! Glory! Cheating such as price hikes will be unheard of! Glory! Honesty will flow so heavy throughout the atmosphere!

Busy streets and people shopping at the beautiful malls. The shopping malls are full of people. Angels are even walking in the malls observing all the activity. There even will be saints who have two mansions one in the new world and another at the cold planet. Yes, have a marvelous time flying around traveling seeing the wonders of God! Glory! Saints are so full of energy ready to travel! The snow is beautiful on the cold planet. Blankets of fresh snow all year long and when it melts, more snow will fall! The snow depths shall be 12 feet or more! It is beautifully white. The Saints love the snow and children love to play in the snow. Jesus makes His appearances on the cold planet. Jesus lets His children know He is right there with them. He will never leave them nor forsake them! It will be so wonderful for families and the Saints to set around the fireplace and sing songs in worship to the Lamb of God as the snow falls outside. You must know traveling for the Saints is much faster than the former world. This is part of God's plans.

CHAPTER 15

The Truth of the Matter

I know what I write in this book sounds amazing and hard for some people to believe. In our world today people are limited to what is going on in this world. Some feel the life we live here in this world is all we going to see! Living in a world full of violence, evil and sin! I want you to know God has better plans than what you see in this world. God desire a world full of life, busy streets, people shopping in malls, children running around playing, people exercising running marathons, ski on the snow and water ski on the sea. People decorate mansions and build fabulous towers high into the sky. Schools and universities teaching so much education. People are laughing and having a good time. They drink fresh juices from the plants. No intoxicated drinks of any kind! No type of smoking! All live healthy, clean lives! No sickness any negative thought! People will be satisfied living in a world with no fear!

Even the animal kingdom will be at peace with no harm to any of them! Everything God create will live through eternity for death does NOT exists! Neither does accidents and injuries exists! There will be no such thing as a negative thought coming to someone to push some off a high cliff, or put some poison into their drink, steal some merchandise out the store, fight that person on the street, talk profanity. None of these thoughts will ever exists in this world. Just pure love for one another for all races of people. This world will be full of all races, nationalities of people all speaking different languages! Every Saint will be empowered with the ability to talk fluently in every language. They will understand each other no matter what language they speak. This is when the song the Saints would sing on former Earth *If Everybody Had Jesus What a Wonderful World It Would Be* comes a reality.

It will be a world full of people, busy streets, malls full of people. In the country it will be people raising crops and giving the Lord the praise! They are riding the Tractor singing songs glorifying Jesus! There are many activities going on! It will NEVER be a dull moment. There are many exciting trips! The Saints will take trips into outer space into the unlimited wonders of God! Yes, taking a space trip without a space capsule or space suit! They will be flying by the power of the Holy Ghost! So many solar systems and planets to visit! All of this fascinate the Saints!

The Lord God will open His many surprises for all His Children. As the Scripture says in **I Corinthians 2:9** But as it is written: *"Eye hath not seen, nor ear heard, neither have entered into the heart of man the things which God hath prepared for them that love Him."* These trips will greatly surpass the artificial trips of roller coaster rides on former Earth. You will be high up in the air with no fear of falling! No fear of suffocation for the Lord God will provide air for all His children to breathe no matter where they may be. This world will be full of glory. Saints celebrating birthdays after birthdays for centuries and centuries to come. One Saint will be saying I am nine thousand years old and still going strong! Living all through eternity full of youth! Enjoying great health for it is IMPOSSIBLE for you to feel bad! That is right IMPOSSIBLE!

All conversation will be positive! It will be impossible to start any conversation which will cause division! Just SMILES OH happy SMILES! True SMILES on the inside and it shows on the outside! All races, nationality will be enjoying each other. There will be no such thing as respect of a person because of the color of their skin. Mentally Handicap individuals who died in former Earth at an early age Jesus interceded and sanctified & Filled with the Holy Ghost are living in riches in this new world. Yes *Emmet Till, Michael Donald* are present in this new world. Those who were murdered lynched just because they were Black in race. *Caucasians, Africans, Chinese* etc young people who were murdered. They died young not given a chance to live their life on former Earth. Through Grace of God Jesus intercedes to sanctify and baptized them and fill them with the Holy Ghost and Fire to get them ready for Heaven and the new world.

Those four black school girls who died in the bombing of 16th Street Baptist Church in Birmingham, Alabama September 15, 1963. Jesus interceded and now they lived in Heaven and are in the new world. I understand it is terrible sad for a stray bullet to end the life of a young person due to a senseless shooting among drug dealers, street violence or gang members. Look at all those young people who lost their lives in World War I and II. Young people who die due to starvation, sickness, or etc. Sweet Jesus will take them, sanctify and fill them with the Holy Ghost to get them ready for Heaven and the new world to come. Jesus loves the little children of the world. The senseless killings of individuals due to the color of their skin, nationality will be judged by God. This includes the murders done by *Slave owners, KU Klux Klan, Prison Officials, Police officers, medical personnel, Black Panthers, Governments* etc. will all be judged by God. Some of these innocent victims will be present in eternity in the new world to come. This is to fulfilled the Scripture spoken by Jesus **St. Matthew 20:16** *"So the last shall be first, and the first last: for many be called, but few chosen."* Those who were treated badly in former Earth are considered last and now honored greatly and those who were considered first such as the wealthy, Kings, world leaders and those with fabulous careers are living in luxury in former Earth are now suffering in the lake of Fire for eternity because they trusted in their worldly possessions more than Jesus. Remember what Jesus said about the Rich man and the beggar Lazarus in **St Luke 16:19-31**. The Rich man enjoy life and would not show any compassion on Lazarus. This happens over and over in our world today. The Rich has plenty of luxury enjoying their air conditioning during summer months, eating ice cream, drinking alcohol, having parties, going to amusement parks, beaches, picnics. They are dressed in fine clothes. They are enjoying eating steak, fried chicken, shrimp, collard greens, spinach, corn etc. The beggar suffering in rags don't have good food to eat. The Rich man would not give the beggar any food for he desired to eat the crumbs which fell from the Rich man table. The Rich man turn the dogs on the beggar and the dogs came and lick his sores. (Dogs has a medication in their saliva to heal wounds.) How many times you have people who have good food or money refuse to help people stricken in poverty? The government in some countries will allow good food to sit on the shipping docks and spoil rather than send it down to feed the hungry people. All of this is wicked in the eyes of God. The beggar died and didn't have a decent burial but he went to Abraham bosom being comforted.

The Rich man also died and had a fabulous funeral! But in Hell he lifted up his eyes being in torment in the flames seeing Lazarus afar off in Abraham bosom. The Rich man beg for mercy calling for Abraham to send Lazarus to dip his finger in cool water and to cool his tongue for he is tormented in this flame. Abraham reminded him during his lifetime he enjoyed good things while Lazarus suffered evil things. Now the tables are turn and Lazarus is comforted and the Rich man is in torment. That is how it is in our world today. The demonic spirit of greed has taken over where people are only concerned about themselves and those close to them. People are interested in trying to get rich. They want to build big empires in this world! What does it profit anyone to gain this world and mess around and lose your soul?

Our main concerns are to help those stricken by the spirit of poverty. It is important to make sure everyone has the basic needs of life to help them to survive in this world. The Basic needs are: Food, pure water, clean air, medical treatment, education, shelter and jobs. Those who deprive people from any of these services are doing evil in the eyes of God. I do not believe in holding people down or keeping them from advancing up in life! Don't you know by rejoicing in other's success will help you to advance! If a person is selfish and hold people down causing them to suffer. It will cause them to stay down to be able to hold them down.

Just for example on a job you have some employees who don't want to train other employees to do their job. They are afraid they may get ahead of them. They will keep them unskilled in that area so they can remain the leader of the team. In cases such as this neither employee can advance. If they cross train it will make room for advancement. Some people will hold people down because of jealousy. They don't want you to move up. All of that is evil in the eyes of God.

There are some people on certain jobs who will always say something negative about an employee to keep them from advancing to the next level. Some will do it for spite! The employee is working hard coming on time to work each day, performing their job to the best of their ability, do not abuse sick time and dress professionally. In all of this they still do not get advance but some other worker who has not spent much time on the job and have a not so good attendance record gets promoted to the next level. This will cause very low morale on the job and cause people to leave that company to go somewhere else to get advancement.

The same will be in the church if you promote some people and hold down other faithful workers it will cause division among the church. Human nature is to judge saying, "*That person don't deserve that promotion.*" You are basing your decision upon the life that person lived. Sometimes the guilty will fire back with the Scripture where Jesus says in **St. Matthew 7:1** "*Judge not, that ye be not judged.*" This is to justify themselves even though they know they are not worthy for the position due to some iniquity or hidden sin. Some will run over top of it thinking God does not see it. They are in for a rude awakening for God got His time and will let you know you are not getting by.

That is why I preach and teach for all to live right! Our lives are being examined by a Holy God! I understand many Christians are depending heavily on Grace to give them a free pass into Heaven. Grace is NOT an excuse to give you permission to live a sinful life on the Earth saying, "*God is a forgiving God.*" This is a verse many Christians do not talk about is in **Hebrews 10:26** "*For if we sin wilfully after that we have received the knowledge of the truth, there remaineth no more sacrifice for sins,*" **There are many Christians who are guilty of that verse and will NOT enter Heaven!** They continue to sin saying, "*God is a forgiving God!*" These people know what they are doing is wrong, but they do it anyway!

If you want to go to Heaven, Sin in all forms **MUST** go! It is only one way to get rid of it, that is through sincere repentance and being Sanctified through the blood of Jesus. That old inherited sin MUST come out in order for a child of God to enter into Heaven! The truth is how can you have the baptism of the Holy Ghost and Fire if sin still lives in you? Light and darkness do not mix. Neither does oil and water. It is impossible for a Christian to have Jesus and still commit sin! No man or woman can serve two masters. **St. Matthew 6:24, I John 3:5-6**

verses. There are plenty people confessing Christ, but they still commit sin depending on repentance to help them get by. Is that biblical?

You cannot mix darkness with light no matter how hard you will try. So if you want to get to Heaven you MUST serve God with ALL our heart, soul and mind! God wants twenty-four hour a day, seven days a week, all twelve months in the year Christians. If you give God all that time, you will have no time left for Satan and NONE of his works! Just like I stated, earlier the Holiness of God changes not just your inside, but it changes your outside as well. Christians who confess Christ, but show no or very little change on the outside, do not have a strong foundation on for their Faith. Satan can easily come and blow their religion out the window. This explains the reason why these Christians always remain on the altar of repentance and sing songs such as *We Fall Down and Get Back Up! A Saint is Nothing But a Sinner Who Fell Down and Got Back Up.* As long as sin is present, Satan knows you have NO chance of entering Heaven. So he encourages Christians to live their lives just like that! Just like I said earlier, Only the pure in hearts shall see God. **St Matthew 5:8.** Jesus changes your inside and outside!

There are many Christians who confess Christ but their life and dress do not measure up! They try to live like Adam in the Garden of Eden. Listen there is a big difference in Adam and those believers in Christ today. When God created Adam, he was already perfect and knew no sin. He needed no Savior. When Adam sin, he lost his holiness and perfection in God. Jesus come being the Second man Adam. He is the strong man to give us more resisting power to live Holy. We as true believers has Jesus in us to stand up against Satan more than Adam in the Garden of Eden. Jesus the strong man can defeat Satan every time!

When Jesus sanctifies us through the blood that old weakness of the first man Adam goes out and Jesus comes on the inside. Jesus is the strong man which will give us more power to resist temptation. That is how we can live free from sin each day because Jesus is on the inside. Greater is Jesus that is within you than Satan that is in the world. **I John 4:4** Ye *are of God, little children, and have overcome them: because greater is he that is in you, than he that is in the world.* That is what Satan does not want you to know. He wants to keep church people believing they can serve God in sin. We cannot serve God in sin. What many Christians do is to commit sin and run and ask God for forgiveness. They love to say, "*God is a forgiving God!*" Another saying they love is "*I am covered by Grace!*" These are NO excuses for Christians to live careless lives indulging in sin!

What Satan don't want you to know is that if the righteous scarcely be save, where will the sinners and ungodly appear? If the Holy people just make it into Heaven how can those who commit sin enter? **I Peter 4:18** As the old Saints would say, "*If you make it into Heaven, you just going to make it!*" **Eldress Lillie P Williams** a powerful woman of God full of the Holy Ghost and Fire said God showed her a vision that she was climbing a mountain struggling to get to the top. She strives hard and she just made it. God brought that verse of Scripture to her mind. This is to let you know if you plan on going to Heaven you must be careful each day what you say, what you do and how you treat others!

This is why I preach and teach to live right! I know there are those who believe they can slip into Heaven covered under *Grace*. They are in for a rude awakening for *Grace* is NOT there to hide you in your foolishness! *Grace* is giving you a chance to repent and turn from your sin not doing it anymore in this life. A prayer of true repentance is "*Lord forgive me of my sins I will not do it anymore!*" There are many Christians who will NOT pray that prayer because they are afraid of sinning again! So, you say Satan is more powerful than Jesus? That is a terrible disrespect to Jesus! Christians need to wake up! Jesus' blood is powerful to take the appetite or desire of sin out of you! That is Sanctification through the blood of Jesus.

It is important to work your salvation out to the fullest! God is looking for His Son to be living in our soul. That is through sanctification through the blood of Jesus. The blood will give you power to resist every temptation of sin. Jesus will stand up in you to tell Satan, "*No! What I have been I am not that way anymore!*" It will be easy to live right when the desire of sin has been taken out. The appetite for sin is gone out of your soul. You don't want to sin. You don't because you don't want to! The blood of Jesus writes your name in the Lamb's Book of life. We can sing the song: O the Blood O the Blood Holy Blood Done Signed My Name Up in Heaven. God wants to look down on Earth and see His children walking everyday in the Word of God. That is True Holiness.

The blood of Jesus gives all of the Saints eternal life up in Heaven because it make us pure on the inside. Glory! Just like I stated earlier, we are pure in heart and only the pure in heart shall see God. **St Matthew 5:8** The blood of Jesus gives us a Mansion up in Heaven. This includes all the righteous things we do for Jesus serving mankind while on Earth. It pleases God for us to do righteous deeds from a pure heart. Sow good seeds, for we will reap what we sow! God will reward us for all the good that we do while we are on Earth. That is the reason I love doing what is right before God. Each day I love to live right walking in the Word of God. I know God is watching and He hears all I say and sees all I do. I love Holiness! If people do not love Holiness how do you expect to enter the Kingdom of Heaven for God Almighty is Holy! Glory! I Peter 1:16

It is God's plans to have solar systems with worlds full of people who will live Holy before Him. Yes, many Planet of Earths full of people, creatures of all kinds with Sun that shines doing the day and moon at night. Farmers will be raising fabulous crops of corn, string beans, rice, wheat, collard greens, kale, spinach and cabbage. On these Planets there will be one Temple for all to come and worship the Almighty God up in Heaven. Jesus shall make His visits to these many Earth like Planets. All will be glad to see Him along with the Angels!

All the Saints will be able to visit these many worlds of people. God will create both male and female. Those Saints from the former Earth God will allow them to enter these worlds to raise families and enjoy having children especially when they had no children on former Earth or their child died or had a handicap! God will give these Saints pleasure to serve Him in these new worlds. Those who had wonderful Christian marriages on former Earth and both individuals made it to Heaven. The Lord God will allow them to marry and go to the new world to live throughout eternity! All will live in riches and be so wealthy in gold, silver, oil and diamonds. The Lord God will bless all these worlds and say, "*Be fruitful and multiply filling up the Earth!*" Man shall marry just like former Earth. One man marry one woman for life! They shall have many sons and daughters all healthy and strong. There will no such thing as Adultery or Fornication! No Transgender, Homosexuality and Lesbianism. Stealing, robbery or rape will be unheard of! Everyone shall live forever for there will be no such thing as death or sickness! Glory! Just like I stated earlier, you will all be at the age of thirty-three years old and that is how you all will live throughout eternity. These worlds will have major cities with tall skyscrapers made of precious metals along with gold. Inventions of flying cars, electric cars which run the highways. Subways, buses and trains will serve as mass transportation. Traffic lights, walk signals, Stop signs and other highway signs will be obeyed with upmost care. Accidents will not exists! There is no need for police, military, jails or prisons. Righteousness and Holiness will prevail all through the land!

Children will be born in Holiness. The women will enjoy having birth with no pain! The baby will be so nice and will not cry! Children will be obedient to their parents. Parents will be teaching them to love the Lord God up in Heaven. The whole world will go up in worship unto the Lord God up in Heaven! Even the creatures will bow in worship. The Lord God will look at all His work and He is well pleased! During the night He shows His smiling face upon the worlds! All the People are so excited to see the Almighty God's smiling face! They shall bow and worship the Almighty! Angels who are so excited will enjoy traveling around to visit the many worlds! There will be many nations speaking many languages, many Holy Kings, Queens, Emperors, Presidents all chosen by the people. Each election in all the worlds will carried out with so much love! Whoever wins the whole nation will rejoice giving a big celebration and all is invited. Love is all through the air and hatred is unheard of! There is no such thing as getting into a fight. That will be unheard of for there will be peace in ALL these worlds!

How would you like traveling on the highway and the people honk at you saying, "*Glory, Hallelujah! Praise the Lord!*" That is doing a traffic jam! There is so much patience doing a traffic jam for all the people will be singing a song to the Lord God up in Heaven or talking on the phone to someone. All conversations will be holy talking what is positive to encourage someone. Negative, gossip and backbiting will not exists! There will even be some who are listening to inspirational Holy Ghost music on the radio. It is glory hallelujah during the traffic jam! Glory, hallelujah at home fixing a meal. Glory, hallelujah at night before you go to sleep! Glory, hallelujah wake up in the morning to go to work or school. Every day will be walking and talking with God Almighty! Hallelujah!

These worlds shall have four seasons just like the former Earth. Spring, summer, fall and winter. All the people will enjoy every one and give God the praise! They will be praising God planting flowers in the spring, mowing grass in the summer, raking leaves doing the fall and enjoying the snow doing the winter. All the people will go to the very large temple and worship the Lord God! It will go up as a sweet smelling fragrance unto God up in Heaven. It pleases God so much for to see all these worlds walking in Holiness unto God! He blesses all of them and the Holy Ghost travels all through the different worlds. All the people will worship the Lord God in one accord! Yes, these worlds will be free from anything negative!

All businesses, companies, neighborhoods, schools, colleges, universities will all be filled with Holy Ghost filled people loving the God of the Heaven in Holiness! A person can be walking in the streets and see someone heading to work praising God! It is normal to see people dancing praising God in the streets! The telephone rings and the business person greets you saying, *"Praise the Lord good morning! God is so wonderful! Glory Bless His name!"* They will go on with the business enjoying the Lord! These worlds will be the one where the Almighty will allow them to speak His Holy name! The reason sin has NOT contaminated this perfect environment! These worlds shall speak the powerful name of the Almighty and it will cause a Spiritual earthquake to shake the people and there will be a wonderful shouts of praise toward God! Even all the creatures shall bow in reverence toward the Almighty! Dancing and praising God! It will be normal for the car to stop aside the road and the person get out and do a dance before God Almighty! Praise the Lord! The Football, baseball, soccer fields, in the middle of their games, they will pause and worship the Lord God Almighty! Yes, the ball game will pause and the players, team members and audience goes up in a great big dance before God! Glory! Working at the factories the workers pause doing their jobs and do a praise dance before God! Hallelujah! Even eating your breakfast in the morning, lunch at noon or supper in the evening you will bless the Lord God up in Heaven! The people will be drinking wonderful nice clear ice-cold water to quench their thirst! Plenty of water and plenty of food! All people are rich in wealth! Poverty does not even exist! Enjoying life in the fullest for eternity!

This is the power of the Holy Ghost which operates in these new worlds! Holiness will prevail and God will be the only one to be worshipped. Jesus being the KING OF KINGS AND LORD OF LORDS will travel and visit these worlds and the people will be so glad to see Him! When they worship Jesus they are worshipping the God of the Heaven in His Son! Glory! How would you like walking into the Mall and the people be walking by you speaking in Tongues praising God? You go into the store and the clerk will greet you with "Praise the Lord! May I help you?" You will be in the store shopping and you think about the Lord God and holler out a praise! The clerks also shout praises! The people in the mall began to praise God and all go up in a dance before the Lord God! Glory! How would you like going in a big department store like Sears and Roebuck and the salesperson gives you a wonderful deal on a brand new refrigerator and doing the sale both of you all talk about the Lord and the Holy Ghost quickens both of you in the store! You all go up in a big dance! Glory! The car salesperson sales you a car giving you a super deal! You began to shout, "Thank you Jesus!" The car salesperson shouts "Glory! Praise the Lord!" You both began quickening in the Holy Ghost! Everyday will be joy! Not a care in the world! Glory!

Just like I stated earlier as the song goes If Everybody Had Jesus What a Wonderful World It Would Be. These are some wonderful worlds part of God's magnificent plans for His children. Yes, there will be parents to raise children which will grow up and have kids to make the parents to become grandparents then those kids have children the generations will continue and it will continue on and on. It will be normal to have multi-great grandparents all looking good at the age of thirty-three years old.

Communities will work together with love to help each other out. In the country farmers will help farmers on with their crops. There will be no spirit of emulations! All will work together as one! People will work together canning vegetables and fruit preparing for the winter. Others will store vegetables and fruits into the freezer. All will make sure their neighbors are taken care of for the winter. There will be no such thing as laziness, everyone will be active to do their part!

In these worlds there will be no Hurricanes, Typhoons, tornados, violent Thunderstorms, duststorms or floods! The Lord God will send the rain in a gentle way. There will no drought for God will make sure they have proper rain to bring forth fabulous crops! The Lord God shall command the birds, ants, beetles, rabbits, mouse and grasshopper to leave their crops alone. The Lord God shall feed them all with grass seed, fruit and nuts from the forest. The Lord God will make sure the people will have fabulous crops of corn, cabbages, butter beans, watermelons, blackeyed peas and garden peas. There shall be great celebrations doing harvest time in the fall of the year! Farmers and neighbors will be giving God the praise for a wonderful year of harvest! Sweet Grapes from the grape vine will be harvested to make wonderful grape juice to drink. All shall be done to the glory of God.

During the winter the snow will fall covering the ground. The snow could last for weeks or a month. The people will be well prepared eating the can or frozen vegetables and fruit. They have enough for their family and their neighbors all winter. The Lord God shall send snow doing the winter but He will not give them ice or sleet to make things slippery. The snow will provide friction for the people to travel. You may asked, "What will happen when the snow melts?" Great question! Listen the Lord God will command the Earth to absorb the moisture. He will also cause the Sun to evaporate what the Earth does not absorb. Anyway God shall make sure the people will not slip up in no way. In these worlds it is impossible to have an accident.

All of this sounds exciting! That is the reason I preach and teach Holiness warning people to give up the world and all of its pleasures because God has so many wonderful things in store for His children. Faith is believing God even you cannot physically see it! How Satan fool a lot of Christians by showing them what they can see with their eyes. He shows them Hollywood, California, Las Vegas, Navada worldy ballgames, amusement parks, beaches and Casinos. Keep this in mind it is only for a season. What I am talking about is for eternity! Eternity is much longer than sixty, seventy, eighty or more years on the Earth.

Christian women look beyond all what Satan is trying to show you! All the dressing in gold, necklaces, earrings and painting your face worshipping the goddess Jezebel. Christian men look beyond what Satan is showing them about marking your body in tattoos and allowing your hair to grow out long! Look beyond worshipping false religions and doctrines overlooking Jesus as the True Son of God. Know that Jesus is the Only way to Heaven. That is the way of the Cross of Calvary! When Jesus comes in the world goes out! Beware of hypocrites who confess Christ saying, "I have Christ on the inside!" The outside looks like somebody who don't know the Lord God. They are NOT truly delivered. The truth of the matter is this is an INSIDE job. Jesus changes your very heart taking out the desire of sin. It changes your outside. The love of the world goes out! People can see the change in you! It gets you ready for world to come; believe me it will be a fabulous time!

Sad to say the love of many Christians for Jesus has waxed cold. That is the reason you have so many Christians trying to serve God while holding to the world! They try to prove they can love the world and be filled with the Holy Ghost too! If they are so filled with the Holy Ghost why is it they don't have the power to reach God to heal people of deadly diseases such as Cancer, diabetes, and mental problems. I have seen how the ambulance has to carry people out of the church to the hospital. People with alcohol and drug problems are given therapy sessions. God has not changed, but it is the faith of the people which has changed. Christians are more involved in the world more than in the power of the Holy Ghost. Education is big on the people's mind! The love of money is the next thing. We need to go back to the old landmark of fasting and praying. It is time for Holy Living and stop playing with Satan, for he is a snake in the grass. He will not rest until he keep you all the way out of Heaven. If he can't keep you all the way out, he will keep you from the third level or less.

So I encourage you to live everyday in the straight and narrow way! Remain with the faithful few Holy people who walk everyday in the fear of the Lord. As long as you live a life free from sin following Jesus, you can be in that number when the Saints go marching into Heaven.

SUMMARY

Throughout this book we discuss God's plans for His Children. They are wonderful plans and will get better when you actually reach Heaven. Eyes have not seen nor Ears heard all the wonderful things God has in store for His Children. **I Corinthians 2:9** Life does not end at the grave, so don't allow Satan to make you believe once you are dead you don't know anything. Once the last breath goes out in this world your eyes open into brand a new world of eternity. Eternity is without beginning or without end.

In God there is no such thing as death. Death was only permitted by God to put an end to sin on the Earth. The Life we live on the Earth will determine where we will spend eternity. Only the pure in hearts shall see God. **St. Matthew 5:8** It takes Holy eyes to see an Almighty God. No sinner can stand in His presence! In order to face the Almighty, you MUST be Holy! In order to reach this perfection, we must go through God's only begotten Son Jesus Christ. Jesus' Blood will wash us taking out the old Adam's nature of sin, so we can reach the requirement of Holiness before God. That is the New Birth which is being born again. **St John 3 Chapter, I John 3 Chapter 1-9 verses** The power of the Holy Ghost and Fire seals you up so Satan can stay out! You are preserved in Jesus and Satan cannot come in to contaminate you with any sin!

The Blood of Jesus writes your name in the **Lambs Book of Life**. Only those who truly repented of their sins and are sanctified through the blood of Jesus name is written in this Book. Lukewarm Christians who sin repent and sin again name is NOT there! The Baptism of the Holy Ghost comes on a Sanctified Life. The Holy Ghost dwells in NO sinner.

There are three levels of Heaven First Heaven: the sky, clouds above the Earth, Second Heaven: space where the stars and planets are located, Third Heaven is God's dwelling place which is hid from this world. Once a soul reach Heaven there are three levels: First level for those who just made it into the Kingdom. The one who prayed the prayer of repentance at their deathbed and Jesus intervene sanctifying them allowing them to enter the Kingdom of Heaven. The Second Level which those who were truly save but grieve the Holy Ghost allowing the spirit of Jezebel to take advantage of their Christian life. The Third Level which is where the New Jerusalem made for those who were faithful in all things written in the Holy Scriptures! Those who dedicated their entire life unto the Lord ever since they were a child. They lived their life Holy before God never using *dope, tobacco, alcohol,* committed *adultery* or *fornication* any time during their life. When you see the third level and all the beauty you now understand why those Sanctified Preachers teach and preach like they did while on Earth.

The Tabernacle not made with hands is so fabulous. The Throne of God has brilliant colors very bright seven times beautiful than any rainbow or fireworks display! It is something the Saints always love to gaze into. Heaven is beautiful full of activities, streets loaded with Saints. There are beautiful Mountains, crystal clear rivers, lakes and streams. God magnificent face shines throughout the levels of Heaven giving it light. The marriage of the Lamb of God to the church will take place in Heaven. That is when Jesus will marry the church. God will perform the wedding. Jesus takes the church to reign for a thousand years upon the Earth during the Millennium. Satan and all the fallen angels will be bound for a thousand years in the bottomless pit. The sinners are cast into Hell and there are sections of Hell prepared for those who commit certain sins. Hell is prepared to punish those who commit sins upon the Earth, such as the sins of the flesh: *Adultery, fornication, hatred, envy, strife, emulations, lasciviousness, uncleanses, Idolatry, witchcraft, variance, heresies, envying, murders, drunkenness, reveling. Homosexuals, lesbians* and *transgenders.* There they shall stay until the dreadful **Day of Judgement**.

After the Millennium the battle of Armageddon. That is one last battle with Satan and the fallen Angels. The Almighty will judge the wicked in the Second Resurrection along with the antichrist and Satan and the fallen angels. Satan and all the rebelling angels shall be struck with eternal blindness and they will be cast into the lake of Fire where the false prophets, antichrist and wicked are located.

There are two resurrections: the Resurrection of the Righteous which will be the rapture of the church. That is when God shall raise an incorruptible body for all the Saints who are present with Him in Heaven from these earthly bodies here on the Earth. Those who are alive and remain shall be changed in moment, twinkling of an eye. Mortal shall put on immortality.. The Saints shall be taken up into Heaven to prepare for the Marriage of the Lamb. The Second Resurrection takes place when God shall call all the sinners up from the graves and Hell and they shall be judged along with Antichrist, false prophets, Satan and the fallen angels.

The Righteous shall go into eternity to live on a new Earth and Heaven where dwell righteousness. This world will be without sickness, accidents, negative thoughts, or doing anything evil. It will be impossible to think of anything negative or evil. We are married to the Lamb of God. All Saints shall be rich in gold, silver, diamonds and pearls. The spirit of Poverty will not exist! Saints shall be celebrating birthdays of hundreds, thousands and millions of years old! They all will be looking like that age of thirty-three years old. Shopping malls, businesses shall be busy with crowd of people. All business will be managed by honest Saints who love each other. Greed and selfishness will not even exist! People walking by shouting, *"Praise the Lord Saint!"* It is impossible for you to feel bad! Nothing contrary to God's perfect Will is around.

Saint will even travel to the cold planet where they can ski on the mountain slopes covered with snow. Children can play in the snow and build fabulous igloos to shield them from the snow. The cold planet will be busy with activity. Many shopping malls crowded with people. People driving snow mobiles and subways running through major cities on the cold planet. All the Saints will be enjoying life and Gabriel blows His trumpet and they all stop what they are doing and exit in a flash back to the New Earth to go the Temple to worship the fabulous Lamb of God and God the Father who sits on the Throne. They will be shouting, dancing and praising God! Their praises shall go up to Heaven before the Almighty as a sweet-smelling savor!

The Almighty shall be so delighted, He will call His children up into Heaven to be in His presence. Jesus will take the bride up to Heaven to be with His Father! Mighty worship will be going on with the Angels of Heaven. Mary the mother of Jesus leads the church in praise and worship. *Mahalia Jackson* sings a glorious song to the Almighty! Many of the Saints sing solos unto the Almighty and the Lamb of God. When the Church sings songs unto the Lamb of God the Angels are quiet because they need not a Savior! So, the Saints sing songs the Angels cannot sing! There will be much dancing, shouting and praising God!

The Almighty shall speak more of His many plans He has for His children. He speaks of solar systems with planets rotating around each a bright Star able to sustain life. There will be many worlds full of people, creatures and living creatures with NO evil, accident, sickness or nothing negative. I will say this is the pure truth NOT a dull moment in Heaven! God's plans are so exciting that this book is a very small glimpses of His magnificent plans!

NOTE FROM THE AUTHOR

I understand this book is hard for some people to believe. This is a Glimpse of God's Plans for His people. God's perfect desire is to have a world where there will be no evil what so ever, not even a negative thought. Just righteousness, joy and peace! Some people may say that is boring because they love a world with some type of violence. They want the violence to stay under control. That is how Satan will fool you. You give an inch to Satan, he will take a mile! Some violence will turn into something big such as mass homicides or multiple murders, rapes, sexual assaults. That is because Satan is NOT your friend. Jesus is your true friend who will deliver you out of your troubles.

Jesus will give you victory over sin and cause you to love righteousness. I love a world with no violence, thefts, rapes, murders and sexual assaults. There is no gambling, card playing or drinking alcohol or smoking cigarettes. There is no divorce and remarriage. I love to please God by marrying someone who NEVER was married before and be married to that one person for life.

Just know in this book subjects will be explained in detail, so you will get a clear understanding why I may sound repetitive that you may know without a shadow of doubt what God's desire for His people to do to please Him. I talk about subjects that other Christian writers may avoid. I will talk about many things the Lord showed me such as once God showed me a vision of me standing in Heaven talking with some church members I knew *Brother Henry Spence, Brother Willard Barkley* and *Brother Samuel Thomas* and we were in the spirit.

I hope you will be blessed as you read this book. May God bless you!
Elder William D Holmes Author

CREDITS

https://www.freeimages.com/photo/box-1-1545557
https://www.biblegateway.com/
https://www.kingjamesbibleonline.org/
https://www.instaencouragements.com/blog/16-names-of-god-and-what-they-mean
https://www.crosswalk.com/blogs/debbie-mcdaniel/50-names-of-jesus-who-the-bible-says-christ-is.html
https://www.thespeakingmom.com/32-names-of-the-holy-spirit-used-in-scripture/
https://www.maxpixel.net/
https://www.openbible.info/topics/jezebel

ABOUT THE AUTHOR

William Dennis Holmes was born on September 27, 1963, to Floyd and Lizzie Mae Holmes in Greensville County, Virginia. He attended Greensville County Public Schools and graduated in June 1982. He grew up in a Christian home with a praying mother and father. They went to a powerful sanctified Holy Ghost—filled church called Rising Sun Holiness Church of Emporia, Virginia, under the leadership of Eldress Lillie P. Williams. It was there along with other churches under Pastor Mother Williams that William Holmes witness the supernatural power of God working among the saints of God. William would see how devoted his mother was to serving God and how she put in him to love the Lord and serve him with a perfect heart. She would pray faithfully calling on God from her bedside. She would talk to him about Jesus. His father would provide for them and love them. He would read the Bible to them at night. His father would also pray.

When he went to church, he saw the saints of God acted the same as his mother and father. He concluded that this was real because they held up holiness more important than education or anything else in this world. They were happy people to be free from the world of sin. They gave up the world and dress and look like the saints of God. They kept their testimony year after year. William knew these people were real.

When William was six years old, he was stricken with a serious illness and placed in Medical College of Virginia Hospital Richmond, Virginia. His father called Mother Williams, who prayed for him, and God wonderfully brought him out. Even the doctors who attended his case said, "It was the hand of God that brought him out." William devoted his heart to the Lord and got saved, sanctified, and baptized of the Holy Ghost filled and fire at the ages of thirteen to fourteen years old. He was nourished in the Word of God under his pastor, Bishop William H. Easter, who succeeded Mother Williams as pastor of Rising Sun Holiness Church of Emporia, Virginia, along with Bishop Rufus A. Easter, pastor of New Jerusalem Holiness Church of Garysburg, North Carolina. God wonderfully worked in his life and took him through many trials and tests. He remained steadfast in the faith and rejoiced in the Lord. He did not cause the church to be ashamed of his conduct. He lived a saved, sanctified life no matter how people treated him. He was called into the ministry and preached his trial sermon October 1990 at New Jerusalem Church under the leadership of the Former Eldress Rosa Banks.

On June 5, 1993, he was united in Holy Matrimony to Velvet L Mangum-Holmes, and God has blessed them with a beautiful marriage. William Holmes joined the United States Navy Reserve in February 2000 and served in Operation Liberation of Kuwait in 2003. William completed in March 2020 twenty years with the United States Naval Reserve. He established an International Prison Ministry in the year of 2005, which is a great blessing to many prisoners across the United States and around the world. He along with Sister Velvet hosts a prison ministry show on radio to reach many prisoners. They send Bibles and other religious materials all free to prisoners, and they make personal visits to inmates preaching the gospel. In the year of 2010 William Holmes graduated from ECPI University with a bachelor's degree in criminal justice and minor in computer science. He currently pastors a church in the Richmond, Virginia, area where he resides. He is also the author of the book titled *A Healthy Christian That Pleases God*, which gives you a clear picture of God's standard of holiness. He also author of other published books. He is beginning a career with the Grace of God to teach in the local Schools helping to educate the next generation.

www.ingramcontent.com/pod-product-compliance
Lightning Source LLC
Chambersburg PA
CBHW021629120626
46545CB00002B/462